GALAPAGOS
The Lost Paradise

GALAPAGOS

The Lost Paradise

PETER SALWEN

THE IMAGE BANK®

ISBN   0941267-12-1

Printed and Bound in Spain

The Author dedicates this book
to Alice and Ira,
two of his favorite explorers.

Written by: Peter Salwen

Produced by: Ted Smart
Edited by: Terri L. Hardin
Design by: Sara Cooper
Photo Research by: Edward Douglas and Annie Price

Boobie Bird

Pinta

Marchena

Frigate Bird

Land Iguana

Fernandina

Cactus Finch

Bo

Pinzon

Santa Cruz

Tree Crab

Finch

Isabela

Red Crab

Tortoise

Marine Iguana

Cormorant

Genovesa

Killer Whale

Grey Shark

Humpback Whale

Mangrove Crab

San Cristobal

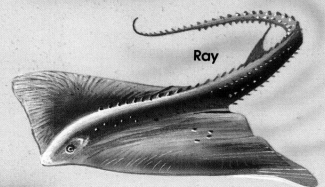

Ray

Española

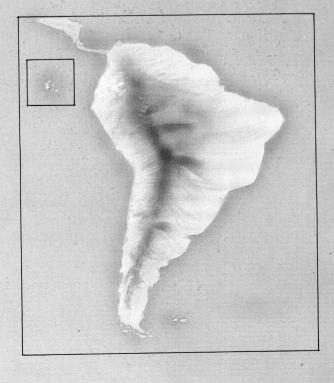

DISCOVERY

There are places in the world whose names alone carry profound meaning, far beyond the mundane facts of their physical reality. The Galápagos archipelago is such a place: for many, it is a symbol of the origin of life on earth as well as its troubled future.

In the earth's geologic history, the Galápagos Islands are about twoscore specks of volcanic rock in the Pacific Ocean, straddling the equator about 600 miles west of Ecuador. In the history of human thought, however, they represent one of the great watersheds in science and philosophy, if for no other reason than having been visited in 1835 by a twenty-six-year-old British naturalist named Charles Darwin.

Darwin observed the islands' uniquely diverse, yet clearly interrelated animals and plants (especially the giant tortoises, iguanas, and finches) and used those observations in building his epoch-making theory of evolution. Before Darwin's visit, those who speculated about man's origin and place in the world groped for a coherent organizing principle; after it, they would be equipped, however imperfectly, with the concept and theory of adaptation and evolution by means of natural selection—a theory of such intellectual power that it still guides students of life a century and a half later.

As Darwin suggested, the "unbroken ocean"

The Galápagos archipelago is a relatively "young" group of islands—between two to three million years old—and they were formed by volcanic eruption. There are still some active volcanos, and they continue to re-form the islands' terrain. Very little grows on the stark, barren rocks at sea level. This page, clockwise from the left: Daphne Minor Island; a highlands' view from Santa Fé Island, with Scalesia helleri (which is endemic to the Galápagos) in the foreground; the surf pounding on the rocky coasts of Española (Hood Island). Opposite page: Pinnacle Rock juts out into the ocean on Bartolomé Island.

was indeed spread out here until sometime between two and three million years ago. Then the islands, which actually are the peaks of undersea mountains, began to surge up from the ocean floor in a series of volcanic eruptions—a process that continues today. In area, they total about 3,000 square miles of basaltic lava rock, scattered over 23,000 or so square miles of ocean. Isabela Island, at 1,803 square miles, is the largest by far. There are four others of fair size—Santa Cruz, Santiago, San Cristóbal and Isabela's neighbor Fernandina—eleven smaller ones, and scores of islets and rocks that barely break the surface.

Their volcanic nature is unmistakable. "In many places the coast is rock-bound, or, more properly, clinker-bound," Herman Melville wrote; "tumbled masses of blackish or greenish stuff like the dross of an iron-furnace, forming dark clefts and caves here and there, into which a ceaseless sea pours a fury of foam." Approaching land, the visitor is greeted by these rocks, here angular and jagged, there twisted into fantastic shapes formed when the upper surface of the still-flowing, plastic lava formed a crust that twisted and buckled before freezing into its final form. "I scarcely hesitate to affirm, that there

must be in the whole archipelago at least two thousand craters," Darwin wrote. "Nothing could be less inviting than the first appearance."

The large islands consist of one or more shield-shaped volcanoes, ranging up to 5,600 feet high (Volcan Wolf on Isabela). Surrounding them are lava flows, cinders, enormous fields of razor-sharp clinker scree, or blocks and layers of black or

Sea mammals, such as the Galápagos sea lion (Zalophus californianus wollebaeki) and the Galápagos fur seal (Arctocephalus galapagoensis), rear their young on the eroded shelves of shoreline. This page, clockwise from top: Sea lions bask on eroded tuff; *the fur seal grotto at James Bay, Santiago (James Island), where it is possible to reach out and stroke the seals, which can be quite friendly; mother sea lion and pup sleep; sea lion at sunset. Opposite page: Sea lion swims at Punta Espinosa, Fernandina Island.*

This page, clockwise from the top left: Young sea lion bulls play-fight on Santa Fé; mother grooms pup; sea lions at skiff on South Plaza Island; sea lions enjoying the sun. Opposite page: Young sea lion pup (Zalophus californianus wollebaeki) sleeping on rocks, Española (Hood Island), top; a sea lion roars (bottom).

dark gray or brown lava, varied here and there with crystals of green olivine, and weathered in places to a dull brick red. The central vents of the larger volcanoes—Wolf and Alcedo on Isabela, La Cumbre on Fernandina and about eight others—have collapsed catastrophically, forming huge *calderas* as much as eight miles in diameter and ringed with near-vertical walls hundreds of feet high. Their slopes are pocked with hun-

dreds of "spatter cones" a few yards in height, each representing its own brief eruption sometime in the fiery past.

All but two or three islands are now volcanically dead, but the active ones can still put on an awesome show. Isabela and Fernandina Islands together make up one of the world's liveliest volcanic regions: there have been fourteen major eruptions on them in this century. In June 1968, after a series of violent earthquakes, the four-mile-wide summit caldera of La Cumbre erupted explosively, and the caldera floor, already 2000 feet deep, suddenly dropped—in some places, by as much as a thousand feet. Though few were there to see it, it ranked as one of history's more spectacular volcanic events. Since then there have been two eruptions in 1979, one in 1982, another in 1984, and the most recent in September 1988: the island-building forces are still conspicuously at work.

In contrast to all this fiery geology, the weather in the Galápagos is surprisingly cool and dry—as much a far cry from the popular notion of "tropical" climate as is the presence of such typical

the trip passively and accidentally, especially those that arrived by sea, either free-floating or on a natural raft such as a log or a mass of matted vegetation.

What kind of creatures were these? To begin with, they had to be species that could survive prolonged exposure to seawater. Mammals have high metabolic rates and need plenty of food and water; very few could have made the trip alive. Likewise, amphibians and freshwater fish must maintain a delicate osmotic balance with their aquatic environment; they would have died before they got out of sight of the mainland. Reptiles, on the other hand, need little fresh water to live, and their hides, being armored with scales or plates, are relatively impervious to salt water. Insects and spiders, too, had a better chance of living to make a successful landfall.

Colonization by these means is a chancy business, but then it doesn't take all that many direct hits for it to work. Ian Thornton, a British

This page at the top left: Sea lion (Zalophus californianus wollebaeki) on the beach. Sea lions are distinguished from seals by their ears and coarser fur. Clockwise from the middle: Humorously clumsy on land, the sea lion is a graceful and swift swimmer. Opposite page: The beauty of these sea mammals (top and

bottom) underwater is awesome. Sea lions are gregarious, but they are also somewhat territorial. A sea lion bull can be dangerous.

First Arrivals

Beginning as sterile masses of hot lava, the primordial islands were soon colonized by plants and animals from the South American mainland. Sea birds were the first arrivals, and perhaps land birds probably carried far to sea by storms. The first plants most likely arrived with them, either as seeds within the birds' intestinal tracts, or as burrs or spores attached to feathers or feet.

Early animal arrivals would have included such strong swimmers as sea lions, fur seals, penguins and sea turtles, helped on their way by the prevailing north- and west-trending currents. But the most intriguing colonists are the ones that made

polar representatives, penguins. Two strong ocean currents that meet just north of the archipelago rule its weather. From May to November or December, the South Equatorial Current, an arm of the north-flowing Humboldt Current, chills the air and wraps the mountaintops in dense fog and a windy drizzle—locally called *garua*—that can persist for days or weeks. From January through April a south-flowing current, called *El Niño*, "The Child," because it often turns up around Christmastime, brings warm tropical water from the Gulf of Panama; the resulting "rainy" season brings warm air and generally bright weather punctuated with occasional heavy downpours.

But the currents and winds of the equatorial eastern Pacific are notoriously capricious. In some years El Niño is weak or fails to appear at all; in those years there is no rainy season. So while higher parts of the larger islands are often wrapped in continuous clouds and dampness, the lower areas and the smaller islands are quite devoid of moisture outside of the January-to-June "wet" season, and are virtual deserts. To Melville, the "special curse" of the Galápagos was this lack of seasonal change: "Cut by the Equator, they know not autumn, and they know not spring; while already reduced to the lees of fire, ruin itself can work little more upon them."

zoologist who did important research in "Darwin's Islands" in the 1960s, has estimated, for instance, that it would have required no more than five successful journeys every million years to account for the existence of the present Galápagos reptiles. And that seems to have been what happened. The handful of individuals that survived the rigors of the passage found themselves in a hostile, barren place—but blessedly free of the predator species that had interfered with their success at home. They adapted themselves over the millennia to new conditions and food supplies, including whatever fresh arrivals the wind or sea might bring later. Their offspring diversified, giving rise to new races and even distinct species. Occasionally, one of these new varieties would go on in its turn to re-colonize other islands within the archipelago, repeating the process that had first brought them from the mainland.

The net result of all this biological activity is what scientists call an unbalanced or "disharmonic" assemblage of species: the islands' spe-

in Galápagos.

This preponderance of bird and reptile life is common in offshore island groups elsewhere in the world. So are two other features that have long struck visitors: the huge size of some species, especially the giant tortoises, (whose Spanish name, *galápago*, has become associated with the archipelago) are nearly unique in the

world, and the extraordinary tameness of animals that have long evolved in isolation, separated from the old country by hundreds of miles of water, and safe from their ancestors' natural enemies. The only really dangerous predator to come to the islands was man, but even he was slow in coming, until carried there by the same freakish winds and currents that gave the archipelago its unique dowry of plant and animal life.

The Discoverers

A long line of voyagers have had little good to report of the Galápagos, beginning with their first European discoverer, the Dominican friar Tomás de Berlanga, Bishop of Panama. In February 1535, Berlanga was sailing south along the coast of Peru on what he expected to be a rou-

cies represent a minute and specialized sampling of the flora and fauna found on the continental land mass. The Galápagos are rich in reptile and bird species, but there are no native amphibians or freshwater fish. Sea lions and fur seals flourish, but there is only a single native terrestrial mammal, the rice rat.

Among plant species, the ferns, grasses, sedges, mosses, lichens, and species of the asteraceae (sunflower) and amaranthaceae (pigweed) groups—the ones whose reproductive structures travel well by sea—have flourished. Particularly unique to the Galápagos are the forests of *Opuntia* (slow-growing trees of the prickly-pear cactus family) just above sea level and *Scalesia* (trees whose ancestors were probably herbaceous) at mid-elevation.

Other groups that are abundant on the South Pacific mainland—cashew and mahogany species, mints, orchids, acanthaceae, pineapples, and the like—are missing or only sparsely represented. Curiously, the palm, which is found just about everywhere in the South Pacific, does not grow

tine administrative mission for Charles V, when his ship was suddenly becalmed and carried far out to sea by strong currents. After drifting for two weeks, Berlanga and his crew were down to only two days' worth of water when they sighted the islands. A boatload of sailors was sent ashore for water and grass for the horses, but as the bishop reported, "they found nothing but seals, and turtles, and such big tortoises that each could carry a man on top of itself, and many iguanas that are like serpents." By now totally out of drinking water, they headed the next day for a larger island "of monstrous shape." Calms prolonged *that* trip to three more days, and when they finally got ashore, the wells they dug gave water "saltier than that of the sea." They survived on cactus pulp, eventually finding a spring barely adequate to their needs, and sailed away.

Despite these hardships, the good bishop did remark appreciatively on the tameness of the island animals, particularly the birds. On the second island, he noted, there were "many birds like those of Spain, but so silly that they do not know how to flee, and many were caught in the hand." His overall assessment, however, was unfavorable. "On this whole island," the bishop reported to His Imperial Catholic Majesty, "I do not think there is a place where one might sow a bushel of corn, because most of it is full of very big stones, so much so, that it seems as though sometime God had showered stones; and the earth there is dross, worthless, because it has not the power of raising a little grass."

The islands' next visitor, the Spanish pirate Diego de Rivadeneira, was also the first to name

them. (Fray Tomás had not considered them worth the trouble.) Seeking a hideout during the interminable colonial wars, he headed for the "Isles discovered by the Bishop," but he too was trapped in the powerful, shifting currents. Unable to steer a straight course (let alone make land) de Rivadeneira and his men became half-convinced that the islands—if they existed at all—were themselves drifting over the sea. Understandably, they called these elusive islands *Las Islas Encantadas*, or the Bewitched Isles.

It was a Flemish mapmaker, Abraham Ortelius, who first affixed the Spanish term *galápago* ("tortoise") to the group, calling them "Insulae de los de Galopegos" in his *Theatrum Orbis*, the first modern atlas, published in 1570. Around the same time, another Spanish explorer, Pedro Sarmiento de Gamboa, was insisting that Tupac Yupanqui, the tenth and greatest of the Inca rulers, had voyaged to the Galápagos from Peru sometime late in the fifteenth century, bringing back "many black-skinned prisoners, much gold and silver, a

Sea lions (Zalophus californianus wolle-baeki) *nurse their young on the Galápagos' rocky coastlines. They are polygamous—a sea lion bull may have many mates in his "harem." This page, clockwise from the top: Galápagos sea lions on beach at Tower Island; sea lions swim in the shallows; sea lions on beach on Rábida (Jervis Island). Opposite page, clockwise from top: Female sea lion relaxing with pup; a sea lion mother rests while her pup's interest is piqued by winged neighbor; a lone sea lion barks; a sea lion pup nuzzles its mother, begging for milk. Overleaf: Sea lions swim in the waves underwater.*

copper throne, and hides similar to cow hides.''

This posed a tantalizing mystery: had South Americans of the pre-Conquest period come to the Galápagos? An archaeological expedition to the islands in 1953, led by the Norwegian explorer and anthropologist Thor Heyerdahl, yielded fragments of aboriginal ceramics, ornamental clay frogs, and stone tools at several sites on the islands. Heyerdahl concluded that *pre*-Inca mariners from South America had in fact been capable of traveling to and from the islands on rafts, and that as far back as the Coastal Tiahuanaço period (about A.D. 1000-1200), they were using the Galápagos Islands as a fishing outpost.

The English navigators who followed the early Spaniards—renegades and freebooters, for the most part—had better luck. The privateer Ambrose Cowley, in a stolen ship he called *Bachelor's Delight*, used James Bay on San Salvador as a base for raids against the Spanish towns along the coast of Peru and Ecuador. He also found time to chart the islands in the 1680s and christened the smaller ones for his buccaneer colleagues (Bindloe, Ewres); the larger ones he named for the English lords (Albemarle, Wainman,

James II) who helped the pirates flourish.

In 1709, Robinson Crusoe—or rather, his real-life model, the Scottish castaway Alexander Selkirk, recently freed from four years' solitude on Juan Fernandez—paid a visit with his rescuer, the buccaneer captain Woodes Rogers. It was Rogers' pilot, incidentally, the erudite William Dampier, who left us the earliest description of the islands that could be called favorable, appreciatively noting the abundance of fine-tasting pigeons, "Guanoes" (iguanas) and especially tortoises ("They are extraordinarily large and fat; and so sweet, that no Pullet eats more pleasantly").

Later callers at the Galápagos included "Foulweather Jack" Byron, grandfather of the poet, Captain Amasa Delano, a maternal ancestor of Franklin Delano Roosevelt, and Captain Alonso de Torres of the Spanish Armada—who once again renamed all the islands, this time using the opportunity to honor various Spanish grandees. In 1790 the first scientific investigator, the Sicilian Alessandro Malaspina, reached the islands as

master of a Spanish ship. Unfortunately Malaspina was imprisoned upon his return to Spain and his papers likewise languished unread.

Three years after Malaspina, Captain James Colnett remapped the islands for the British Admiralty, which had become interested in the Galápagos as a base and commissary for England's whaling fleet. His reports opened the way to exploitation by whalers, who carried off the giant tortoises by the thousands, stacking them like casks in their ships' holds, to be opened months later for fresh meat.

—◇•◇•◇—

Two-Legged Predators

The first full-time Galápagos resident was a disagreeable Irish sailor named Patrick Watkins, who had been put ashore on Charles Island. Living in a sort of cave scraped out of the lava, he somehow contrived to grow a crop of potatoes and tobacco, which he traded for rum when whalers came a-calling. A fearsome, "beast-like," half-naked creature with wild red locks and beard, Watkins captured stray sailors, holding them until he had amassed a crew capable of carrying him back to the mainland in a stolen boat. En route, however, water ran low (the old story) and Watkins killed his companions one by one. He eventually ended up in jail in the tiny coastal settlement of Paita, having initiated a bloodthirsty epoch in Galápagoan history.

In 1812, Captain David Porter of the U.S. frigate *Essex* hove to at Post Office Bay on Charles Island. Since Colnett's time, a box nailed to a tree had served visiting mariners as a depot. Not a ship passed that way without calling to leave news of herself or, if homebound, to pick up and forward letters left by others. Porter most ungallantly used information from these letters to make war on the British whalers, and succeeded in driving them from that part of the Pacific.

From the naturalist's point of view, Porter's great crime was that of setting ashore four goats from the *Essex* to graze on James (Santiago) Island. They ran off after a week, at which Porter blandly noted, "Perhaps nature, whose ways are mysterious, has embraced this first opportunity of stocking this island with a race of animals who are almost as well enabled to withstand the want of water as the tortoise with which it now abounds." Ultimately, such introduced species would decimate the endemic wildlife on many of the islands.

In the early years, though, the only important predator was man. Fur seals were hunted almost to the point of extinction, but it was the tortoises that suffered worst, with an estimated 100,000 taken, mainly by whalers, by the middle of the nineteenth century. Ships of that pre-refrigeration era had no other way to carry fresh provisions for

This page, top: Sea lion (Zalophus californianus wollebaeki) laying on the shore on Rábida (Jervis Island). Bottom: A school of bottlenose dolphins. Dolphins will often accompany ships, leaping from the water in a graceful, seemingly choreographed ballet. Opposite page: single bottlenose dolphin (top); sperm whale (Physeter catadon) breaching (bottom).

a voyage that—to be profitable—might have to extend over months or even years. Without the natural larder of the Galápagos, it has been asserted that the Pacific whaling industry could not have been possible. Visiting Chatham Island in 1835, Darwin noted, "In the woods there are many wild pigs and goats; but the staple article of animal food is supplied by the tortoises. Their numbers have of course been greatly reduced in this island, but the people yet count on two days' hunting giving them food for the rest of the week. It is said that formerly single vessels have taken away as many as seven hundred, and that the ship's company of a frigate some years since brought down in one day two hundred tortoises to the beach." These depredations literally emptied some islands of their tortoises, and brought the tortoise populations of several others to the brink of extinction.

On February 12, 1832 (which happened to be Darwin's twenty-third birthday), the archipelago was annexed by the recently formed nation of Ecuador and placed under the governorship of the Louisiana-born Ecuadorian General Jose Villamil. He established an outpost, which he called Asilo de la Paz, on Charles Island, populating it with former political prisoners who raised meat and vegetables for sale to passing whalers. Unfortunately, the Government of Ecuador seemed to have somewhat misread Villamil's intentions; they converted his fledgling settlement into a penal colony. By the time of Darwin's visit three years later, the population had grown to

The Galápagos penguin (Spheniscus mendiculus) *is the only "tropical" penguin in the world—all others reside in polar regions, north and south. This page, clockwise from top on the left: Galápagos penguin; penguins swimming off the coast of Bartolomé Island; a penguin surveys the view from its eroded perch; an immature penguin. Opposite page: Galápagos penguin.*

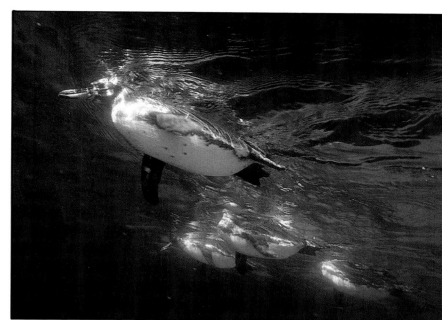

nearly three hundred, almost entirely made up of hardened criminals. Villamil moved on and founded a new settlement on Chatham. He left La Paz in the not-very-peaceable hands of one Colonel Williams, a gentleman much given to flogging and setting dogs on his wards, who ultimately revolted and drove him from the place.

The most illustrious scientific visitor to the Galápagos (though nobody knew it at the time) was of course young Darwin, who arrived in the capacity of ship's naturalist aboard Her Majesty's frigate *Beagle*, then in the midst of a five-year,

round-the-world voyage of exploration and discovery. At the start of the voyage, Darwin had been what might charitably be called a bright but directionless young man. He had thought of studying for the clergy, but found he had little vocation for that; he tried medical school, but learned that the sight of blood made him sick. When the chance to sail as a naturalist came his way, his father objected to such a waste of time. Only by the intercession of his uncle, the pottery manufacturer Josiah Wedgwood, was he allowed, at the last minute, to join the expedition.

Throughout the voyage Darwin suffered horribly (and more or less continuously) from seasickness. Nevertheless he proved himself a tireless, sensitive and observant naturalist, in the great 18th-century tradition of Humboldt and Fabre. He not only recorded and described every species he could lay hands on; he measured, weighed, compared and experimented, examining the feet and guts of land and sea birds, for instance, to learn exactly how different sorts of seeds and spores might have been carried to the islands. He rode on a tortoise and noted its precise speed

(360 yards an hour). More importantly, he thought deeply about what he saw, for he recognized that it was not only the strangeness of the animals that was worthy of notice, but the obvious family relationships among the various species and sub-species. It would not have been "nearly so won-derful," he speculated, to have found some of the islands uninhabited, or inhabited by totally unrelated assemblages of animals and plants. "But it is the circumstance, that several of the islands possess their own species of the tortoise, mocking-thrush [mockingbird], finches, and numerous plants, those species having the same general habits, occupying analogous situations, and obvi-ously filling the same place in the natural econ-omy of this archipelago, that strikes me with wonder." It was such speculations that, trans-muted after nearly a quarter of a century of reflection and further study, emerged to shake the foundations of scientific thought in Darwin's 1859 masterwork, *The Origin of Species by Means of Natural Selection: Or the Preservation of Favored Races in the Struggle for Life.*

A half-dozen years after Darwin came the islands' most illustrious literary visitor: a twenty-one-year-old American seaman named Herman Melville, fifteen months out of New Bedford on

This page, counter-clockwise from the top: The bleak aspect of sea level on Bartolomé Island; shore petunia (Cacabus miersii) in Punta Espinosa, Fernandina Island; Opuntia cacti erupt from a lava bed on Fernandina Island. Opposite page: Pelicans rest in a tree at Tortuga Bay, Santa Cruz Island.

the whaler *Acushnet*—the ship he would later immortalize as Captain Ahab's *Pequod*. Melville listened avidly to the tales of the "daungerous and dreadfull" islands and their godforsaken cast of runaways, castaways and hermits—of buccaneers, of the murderous "Hermit Oberlus" (a.k.a. Patrick Watkins) and the tragic, shipwrecked Chola Widow of Norfolk Isle. A dozen years later, woven through with Melville's own darkly poetic sense

of the tormented islands, they appeared as ten sketches in the pages of *Putnam's*, and were later collected as *The Encantadas or Enchanted Isles*.

In the 1880s another Ecuadorian entrepreneur, Manuel J. Cobos, founded a second colony on Chatham Island, ironically naming it *Progreso* and using slave labor to raise sugar cane and to gather the moss-like *orchilla*, which was sold as a commercial dyestuff. Even crueler and more despotic than Colonel Williams, Cobos was eventually hacked to death by his convict-laborers—on the same spot where, not long before, five of them had been executed on his orders. His village survives today as an agricultural settlement, supplying the islands with bananas and oranges and wild guavas.

Another failed settlement-*cum*-penal colony, on Charles Island, was started in 1870 by one Señor Valdizan; his prisoners, too, revolted and established a reign of terror before returning to the mainland or over to Chatham. In 1893 an eminent Guayaquil lawyer, Don Antonio Gil, also attempted to start a settlement on Charles (which in the interim had been renamed Floreana), thought better of it, and founded the villages of Villamil and Santo Tomás on Isabela (Albemarle).

As the place names in parentheses throughout this story suggest, Galápagos nomenclature has always been a somewhat hit-or-miss business, with various English and Spanish callers bestowing names rather freely on most of the larger islands and many of the smaller ones. Even Captain Porter, the marauding American, named

This page, clockwise from the top: The view from Fernandina Island; the edge of a caldera at Santa Cruz; Opuntia echios gigantea, one of the two varieties of prickly-pear cactus trees which grow in the Galápagos. Op- *posite page: Two views of Volcan Chico in eruption at Sierra Negra at Isabela Island. Overleaf: Volcan Chico lights the night sky with its fiery outbursts.*

one of the islands for himself and another for his first lieutenant, John Downes. Of course, the government of Ecuador has its own views in the matter. In 1892, to honor Christopher Columbus on the 400th anniversary of his first transatlantic voyage, several of the islands were given names associated with the discoverer, e.g., Pinta and Santa Maria, Fernandina and Isabela (for the Spanish sovereigns), and San Cristóbal (for Columbus' patron saint). At the same time the official name of the archipelago was changed to "Archipiélago de Colón"—a name used today by virtually no one.

The result is that the 41 principal islands or islets that make up the archipelago have been known by no fewer than 113 names, mostly but not all English or Spanish—including Nameless (or Sin Nombre) Island, a speck of rock in Pinzón

Channel between Santa Cruz and Pinzón islands.

In the 1920s, the islands were rediscovered, this time by William Beebe, a slender, ebullient New York Zoological Society zoologist and pioneering deep-sea diver with a flair for exploration and an

even greater flair for publicity. His discoveries above and below sea level, recounted in two lavishly illustrated volumes, *Galápagos, World's End* (1924) and *The Arcturus Adventure* (1926), brought the archipelago to the world's attention again. They also brought about a curious and unlikely result: an influx of immigrants from Norway.

For some reason, Beebe's colorful, exotic descriptions seemed to hold a special appeal for Norwegian readers. An unscrupulous Oslo promoter with the un-Nordic name of Harry Randall decided to capitalize on this romance. He flooded Norway with promotional literature touting the "soil so rich that 100,000 people could easily find homes" and the "thousands of trees of every type which bear fruit the whole year around," and succeeded in conning over a hundred of his countrymen, at six thousand *kroner* a couple, to ship out for the islands. Of the first 22 settlers,

The many faces of the masked booby (Sula dactylatra). This page, clockwise from the top left: A masked booby with chick, Tower Island; An adult masked booby and chick, Española (Hood Island); a masked booby gaining adult plumage, Tower Island; masked booby grooming, Española (Hood Island). Opposite page: A masked booby in flight (top); an adult masked booby with chick, Tower Island. Overleaf: Masked boobies can be found on many of the islands. Here they are photographed on Hood (page left, top), Tower (page left, bottom) and South Plaza (page right) Islands.

The terrain of the Galápagos has been and is continuing to be formed by the eruptions of its many volcanos. This page, clockwise from the top: A beach on Isabela Island; Kicker Rock at Stephen's Bay, San Cristóbal Island; a tidal blowhole on Española (Hood Island). Opposite page: The jagged coast of Española (Hood Island) serves as a rookery for the masked booby (Sula dactylatra), among others. Overleaf: Although most of the Galápagos archipelago is uninhabitable, its desolate beauty is compelling.

all but four were gone within six months, twelve of them dying in Guayaquil. Still, they kept coming, another hundred or so over the next two years. Some of them tried to set up a fish cannery, others a coffee plantation and a sugar refinery. Within three years the cannery was gone (boiler explosion) and so were most of the Norwegians—though a few stayed on at the newly established town of Puerto Ayora (Academy Bay)

with two admirers, Alfred Lorenz and Robert Phillipson, and settled near the Wittmers.

No living person knows (or is willing to tell) what tangled relationships evolved over the next two years, but in March 1934 the Baroness and Phillipson vanished mysteriously; the following November Lorenz was shipwrecked and found dead with a Norwegian fisherman on Marchena Island. When he learned of Lorenz's death, four days later, Dr. Ritter took his own life. His wife

left the island soon afterward, leaving her former neighbors to spin many a wild yarn. Several sensational magazine articles and a book, *Satan Came to Eden*, helped to bring the affair to world notice.

During World War II, the Ecuadorian government permitted the United States to use the small island of Baltra—just north of Santa Cruz—as an air base from which to defend the Panama Canal. Unfortunately for the local ecology, the soldiers relieved the boredom by shooting any-

on the south shore of Santa Cruz.

By then, the islands had become, in Victor W. von Hagen's felicitous phrase, "part of a millionaire's grand tour." William Kissam Vanderbilt, Vincent Astor, and a whole parade of wealthy yachtsmen made it their business to drop anchor off Post Office Bay and bring back tales (and, too often, specimens) of the local wildlife. Of this group, Gifford Pinchot, Governor of Penn-

sylvania and founder of the U.S. Forest Service, has left the most engaging account. He was particularly delighted when a land iguana on North Seymour Island actually crawled into his lap to feed on a proffered grasshopper; from then on Pinchot insisted on referring to the animals as "Lap Dragons."

Soon afterwards, Floreana acquired another bit of grisly folklore fully up to Melville's standards. In August 1932, Heinz Wittmer came to the island with his wife Margaret and son Harry. They had as neighbors Dr. Friedrich Ritter, a Berlin dentist, and his mistress Dora Koerwin, who had settled on the island's western slopes six years before. Two months after the Ritters, Eloise Bosquet von Wagner-Wehrborn, the self-styled "Baroness of the Galápagos," showed up

Lava lizards can be found almost everywhere. This page, clockwise from the top left: A lava lizard in a tree; in the underbrush; Tropidurus albemarlensis on Santa Cruz Island; and Tropidurus grayi on Española (Hood Island). Opposite page: A female lava lizard (Tropidurus albermarlensis) on Santa Cruz Island.

The swallow-tailed gull (Creagrus furcatus) breeds mainly in Galápagos. This page, clockwise from the top: The white mark on the adult swallow-tailed gull's beak is thought to make it easier for the gull chicks begging for food in the dark; a swallow-tailed gull in flight; one swallow-tailed gull alights on another; swallow-tailed gull alights on Española (Hood Island). Opposite page: Swallow-tailed gull in flight over South Plaza Island.

thing that moved, and used the outer rocks—and their populations of sea lions—for bombing practice. Today the islands have a permanent population of about 6,000, about half of whom live on San Cristóbal and the rest in settlements on Santa Cruz, Isabela and Floreana. The principal port of call for visitors is Academy Bay, where there are several inns and other tourist facilities, as well as the Galápagos National Park headquarters and the Charles Darwin Research Station.

Naturalists' Paradise

"The natural history of these islands is eminently curious," Darwin observed, in one of the great understatements in scientific literature, "and well deserves attention." Since his day, the Galápagos have been a cynosure for naturalists from around the world. They come to study virtually every aspect of nature, since the archipelago has something unique to offer in every department: geology, climatology, ichthyology, ornithology, herpetology, plant systematics, evolutionary studies, ethology and more. Over three dozen major and scores of minor scientific expeditions have focused on the Galápagos or in-

cluded the islands in their itinerary, and the bibliography of resulting scientific papers by now numbers over a thousand.

Despite the Galápagos' stellar value as an international scientific resource, there was no effort to extend any official protection to the islands until it was almost too late. In 1934 the government of Ecuador designated several of the smaller islands as wildlife sanctuaries, but the law had no effect on predators, two-legged or otherwise.

This page, at the top left: Swallow-tailed gull (Creagrus furcatus) on Tower Island. Top right to bottom: swallow-tailed gull flying over South Plaza Island; swallow-tailed gulls with chick, Española (Hood Island); swallow-tailed gull on Española (Hood Island). Opposite page: Swallow-tailed gull calling, South Plaza Island.

plex of low white buildings that make up the Charles Darwin Research Station. Inaugurated in 1964, CDRS now offers research facilities for up to ten visiting scientists, a well-equipped laboratory and workshop, a late-model motor cruiser, and several large enclosures for the *galápagos*, the giant tortoises that give the islands their name. A small museum stands nearby, named in honor of Dr. Victor Van Straëlen, the Foundation's first president. The station conducts a tortoise breeding and rearing program in an attempt to stave off extinction of several types of tortoise and land iguana, and a bird-banding program to monitor the populations of frigates, boobies, waved albatross and other precarious species, and carries out research in meteorology, seismology (a natural concern) and oceanography.

For many, fieldwork in this remarkable setting has been a prelude to considerable scientific achievement, and the names of such eminent specialists as David Lack, Irenaus Eibl-Eibesfeldt,

By the mid-1950s, however, even casual observers began to recognize how fragile and endangered the islands had become. The idea of a permanent scientific center dedicated to preservation and study of Galápagos wildlife took form soon after with a pair of surveys sponsored by the International Union for the Conservation of Nature and Natural Resources, UNESCO, and the International Committee for the Preservation of Birds, as well as the New York Zoological Society, Time, Inc., and the government of Ecuador. In 1959, the centennial year of *The Origin of Species*, the entire archipelago, except for the few settled areas, was declared a national park. Meanwhile, Sir Julian Huxley, eminent zoologist and grandson of Darwin's principal nineteenth-century champion, had agreed to serve as acting chairman of the Charles Darwin Foundation for the Galápagos Islands, and construction for the Research Station began two years later at Academy Bay, near Puerto Ayora village on Santa Cruz.

Today a signboard in Spanish, English and French marks the entrance to the sprawling com-

Bryan Nelson, Ian Thornton and Robert Bowman are now firmly linked to their work there. To this distinguished roster should be added Tui De Roy, one of the few Galápagos natives (or near-natives, since she went to the islands at age two) to have achieved world renown. Her parents, following their own wilderness dream, left Brussels thirty-five years ago to farm and fish on Santa Cruz, and their daughter's intuitive sympathy with the native wildlife and talent with the camera quickly brought her to the front ranks of the world's nature photographers.

In the past fifteen or twenty years the Galápagos have become a prime tourist destination—a financial blessing and, unfortunately, something of an ecological curse, since the islands now receive somewhere between 40,000 and 60,000 visitors yearly. Several airlines, including Ecuatoriana, Ecuador's national airline, have regularly scheduled flights to Ecuador from New York, Miami and Los Angeles. It is still feasible, though chancy, to fly in and get lodgings at Puerto Ayora, and make island-hopping arrangements locally with any of several reputable boat-owners. Visitors must be accompanied by naturalist-guides, who are trained at the CDRS and will also provide a very helpful pre-landfall briefing before each shore visit. Any good travel agent can put you together with a Galápagos tour operator; nature and conservation organizations, such as the Audubon Society and major zoos and museums, also organize excellent Galápagos tours. The South American Explorers Club, with offices in Lima, Peru, and Denver, is an excellent clearinghouse for up-to-date and candid travel information.

Most group tours, unfortunately, visit only a few islands. Trips ashore are tantalizingly brief, and for most visitors an excursion to one of the

more distant or challenging—i.e., more rewarding—environments is entirely out of the question. With that reservation, it has to be admitted that a Galápagos visit is indeed (to quote one recent promotional booklet) "a brief trip to a paradise that really exists." And there is some solace in knowing that even William Beebe wrote his first book on the basis of a few days' visit.

•◇•◇•

Land iguanas are to be found everywhere in the Galápagos, and are especially expert at begging for food. This page, clockwise from the top: Land iguana (Conolophus subcristatus) on South Plaza Island; land iguana on top of broken lava rocks. Opposite page: A land iguana rests in a gully. Overleaf: A land iguana in close-up, South Plaza Island.

GALÁPAGOS JOURNAL

My own all-too-brief visit to the Galápagos, some years back, resulted indirectly from a series of freelance writing and editing assignments on biology and natural history books. The work brought an intense immersion in Charles Darwin's life and work, and ultimately a longing to set foot on the islands that had affected him so profoundly. Then, one late spring afternoon, a friend at the

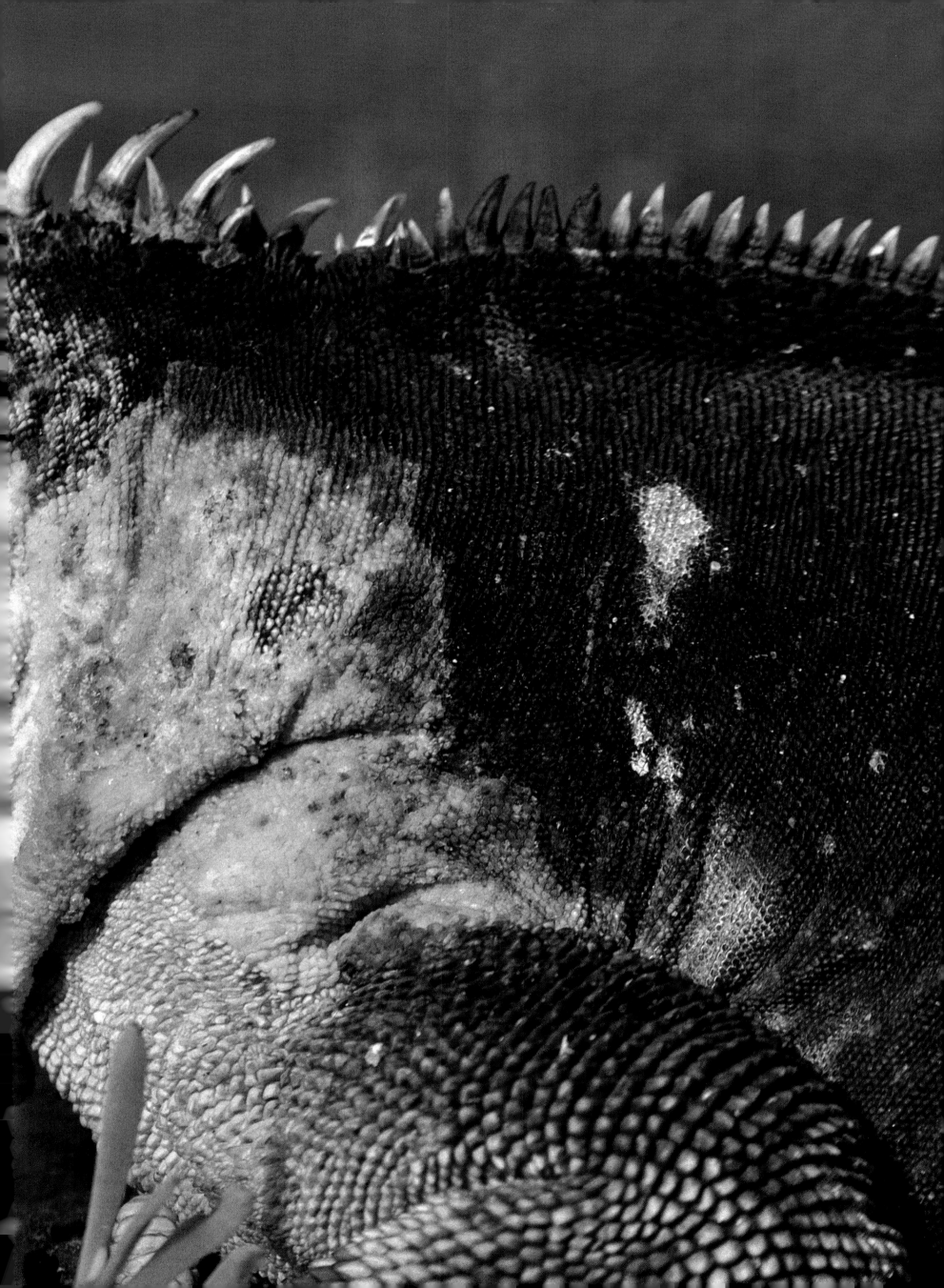

The Galápagos land iguana (Conolophus subcristatus) *is a species endemic to the archipelago. This page, top: The land iguana is a vegetarian. Here, a land iguana is munching a piece of Opuntia, a type of prickly-pear cactus which is quite common throughout the island group. Bottom: Land iguanas from South Plaza Island. Opposite page: The yellowish orange splotches of the land iguana make it easy to spot on barren lava.*

New York Zoological Society called with an offer I had no intention of refusing: a slot had just opened up in the Society's next group tour to the Galápagos! It was to be something of an all-star cruise, packed with ornithologists and other scientific types from the Audubon Society and several research centers, and it had to be filled in a hurry—and at a reduced rate. There was barely time to ask, "Where's the Dramamine?" before I found myself on my way.

Approaching the Galápagos from the east on board the M.V. Iguana. *Our only company since we put out from Guayaquil two days ago has been some Mother Carey's chickens, a pair of blue whales, a shark, and swarms of flying fish that skip along just above the waves for as much as 75 yards at a go.*

The *Iguana*, which sank in Academy Bay a few years after our trip, was originally built for trade in the St. Lawrence River and the coast of maritime Canada. She carried 85 passengers and was typical of the older Galápagos cruisers: rudimentary sleeping quarters, a comfortable saloon

on the main deck, a tendency to wallow in heavy weather, primitive plumbing, and an open topdeck where a few more of us gathered each successive night to sleep under the stars or clouds. Chugging along at 20 knots or so, it took her two and a half days to cover the 600 miles from Guayaquil to the islands.

Our first harbinger of land: a red-billed tropic bird circled us at dawn. Those magnificent, slightly ridiculous tail feathers extended in flight or arched over the water behind him when he settled briefly on the waves to inspect our ship. Just after sunrise we had more visitors: waved albatross, frigatebirds, masked boobies.

Also known as the "man-o-war bird," the frigatebird is one of the animal kingdom's most spectacular fliers. With its light body, seven-foot wingspan and agile forked tail, the frigate can swoop and dart acrobatically, or soar as high as 4,000 feet above the sea. The frigates are also notorious pirates, using their stunt-flying skills to harass and attack other birds while they fish and

These pages: Of the land iguana, Darwin wrote, ". . . they curl their tails, and, raising themselves on their front legs, nod their heads up and down, and to look very fierce; but in reality they are not at all so; if one just stamps on the ground, down go their tails, and off they shuffle as quickly as they can." Land iguanas (Conolophus subcristatus) were once common on many islands in the Galápagos archipelago; now they are found mostly on Fernandina and Santa Fé Islands.*

rob them of their catch.

Hood Island just visible on horizon.

Hood Island, or Española, in the extreme southeast of the group, is unusual among the Galápagos: it is not a volcano, but a roughly eight-by-three-mile block of lava that hardened beneath the sea and was later uplifted to form cliffs, as much as 300 feet high, along its southern shore. Punta Suarez, at the western tip, is home to colonies of sea lions and a unique, brightly colored subspecies of marine iguana. The males are the flashiest in mating season, with bright orange-and-red mottling, green front legs, and a green crest from neck to tail.

We climb into the ship's two 16-foot tenders at Punta Suarez, where we splash and slop ashore to a small beach. The finches greet us with low chirps; the mockingbirds more gaily, circling in for a close inspection and apparently find us acceptable, since one lands on my hat.

Almost every visitor to the Galápagos expresses astonishment at the extreme tameness of the birds, but the mockingbirds are undoubtedly the boldest of all. Darwin told of lifting a tortoise-shell pitcher while a mockingbird, perched on

A wide variety of plant life can be found in the Galápagos Islands. This page, clockwise from the top: An Opuntia helleri or prickly pear cactus blossoms on Tower Island; a mangrove tree on Fernandina Island. Opposite page: A venerable Opuntia stands tall on Rábida (Jervis Island). Overleaf: Galápagos hawks (Buteo galapagoensis) perch on a dead tree in James Bay, Santiago (James Island).

the rim, drank from it calmly. Ornithologist Bryan Nelson found the Hood mockers particularly brazen: "If we averted our eyes from, much less turned our backs on the breakfast table, they jumped up and gobbled the butter, laying their slim beaks sideways to get bigger mouthfuls. Often a tug at the hand alerted us to the forty thieves stealing butter from our bread."

Española's jagged southern shore is also eroded by waves into narrow clefts. One of these, near Punta Suarez, forms an inverted funnel, where the surf collects and is forced into a dramatic blowhole. Even on a quiet day the spume hisses thirty or forty feet skyward. The island supports a good variety of animal species: the beaches, curving eastward in a dreamy arc, are colonized by sea lions, long-billed mockingbirds, Galápagos doves, short-eared owls, oyster-catchers and

This page, clockwise from the top: Cordia lutea, *Santa Fé Island;* Opuntia echios var. gigantea; Scalesia affinis aster, *Isabela Island. Opposite page: The* Opuntia *forests of South Plaza (top) and Santa Fé (bottom)*

Islands. Cacti can be resistant to seawater; it is thought that Opuntia *floated to the islands from the mainland.*

swallow-tailed gulls. Boobies nest on a broad ledge above Punta Suarez, and the area is home to a unique tortoise species with an elegantly curved, bulbous shell.

We take the southward path to the famous blowhole, where spume hisses upward 30-40 feet; then past a quiet, mixed colony of boobies, blue-footed and masked. Inland, the albatrosses are on and near their nests, dancing, moo-calling, skypointing and clashing bills. Majestic birds in flight, but here on their home territory they look regal and comical at the same time.

The endearing, clumsy-looking boobies (their name is said to be a corruption of the Spanish *bobo*, "clown") are a tourist favorite—right up there with the tortoises. They are near cousins to the much more formidable-looking gannets of northern waters and, like the gannets, are strong fliers and spectacular divers. They often fish in small groups, plunging from a height of 50-80 feet into the coastal shallows in a screaming 45-degree dive and emerging with a fish caught in the open bill on the way to the surface. As the blue-foots breed throughout the year, to the delight of the ornithologists in our group, we got to see many of the typical behaviors of courting and nesting couples: parading, jabbing, "sky-pointing" with outstretched, curved wings, and—most startling of all—incubating an egg by embracing it in the webs of those amazing blue feet.

We were extremely fortunate to visit Española during the albatrosses' mating season; this is in fact the world's only breeding population of the

Galápagos waved albatross. The complex mating dance includes an almost hypnotic head-circling and bowing, with much noisy clapping and clattering of the partners' large yellow bills, and loud, hectic, weird calls—an ecstatic display that an observer could easily mistake for fighting.

On the beach, before returning to the Iguana, we get a quick close-up look at the unique Hood marine iguanas, with their patches of bright red. They are nicely color coordinated with the scores of bright red Sally Lightfoot crabs, which share their territory peaceably. Captain says we will pass between Floreana and San

The waved albatross (Diomedea irrorata) breeds only in the Galápagos Islands. This page, clockwise from the top: waved albatross in flight over Española (Hood Island); a young waved albatross; an albatross rookery on Española (Hood Island); a waved albatross chick.

Opposite page: Two views of the waved albatross in flight.

Cristóbal islands overnight and reach Santa Cruz in the morning.

San Cristóbal, or Chatham, is the easternmost of the large islands and the most densely settled. The official capital of Ecuador's Galápagos province is the town of Puerto Baquerizo Moreno, at Wreck Bay (Bahía Naufragio) on the island's southwest tip. (As we passed, we thought we could make out the lighthouse there—the only one in the archipelago.) Another village, Progreso, lies five miles inland and several hundred feet up the flanks of a large volcano. Progreso, once the convict settlement established by the horrible Manuel Cobos, is now a quiet agricultural village. A few tortoises survive in the low north-central area, but elsewhere they have been wiped out by wild goats, donkeys, and pigs, which eat the tortoises' eggs and young. Multi-spired, 486-foot-high Kicker Rock, east of Wreck Bay, is a spectacular home to colonies of boobies and frigatebirds.

Floreana, which slips past our port bow in the night, is the island with the most colorful history: home of Patrick Watkins, the "Fatherless Oberlus," and of the alluring Eloisa von Wagner,

"Baroness of the Galápagos," and her ill-fated associates. Post Office Bay, with the remains of the abandoned Norwegian fish processing plant nearby, occupies an indentation in the northwest shore. Floreana also has some of the Islands' most spectacular settings: the craggy submerged volcano known as "Devil's Crown" (Onslow Island), with its the contorted, cave-pierced cliffs of Las Cuevas Cove, mangrove swamps, flamingo lagoons, and beaches of black or greenish sand.

Made land at Academy Bay. This is the only substantial settlement on the islands, nestled in a protected V-shaped cove on the south shore of Santa Cruz. The approach passes Punta Ayora on the left, where a straggle of houses look out from above the rocky shore. What looks at first like a seal about thirty yards to port turns out to be a swimming marine iguana. The most prominent point, just before reaching Academy Bay, is occupied by a thriving colony of them, with Carl Angermeyer's house directly behind.

In the cool early morning, the cold-blooded marine iguanas splay out their legs in the flat "basking" posture, to soak up a maximum of the sun's warmth. Angermeyer, a German who with his brothers Gusch and Fritz settled on Santa Cruz before World War II, has been called the "Galápagos Crusoe." He is considered something of a philosopher, and over the years he has adopted an understandably proprietary attitude toward the iguanas—he feeds them on table scraps—and about the Galápagos fauna generally. The naturalists aboard the *Iguana* thought he was just awful. ("Angermeyer's been here thirty years, so he thinks the animals are his pets," one of them muttered. "Somebody should tell him the iguanas have been here thirty *million* years.") On the other hand, Dr. Irenaus Eibl-Eibesfeldt, surveying the islands for UNESCO in 1957, retained Angermeyer to guide him up

These pages: Various courtship displays of the male and female waved albatross (Diomedea irrorata) are pictured here. All photographs were taken on Española (Hood Island), where a waved albatross rookery is established. Bottom on the right: Pair of waved albatrosses on nest.

The distinctive terrain of the Galápagos continues to be formed by volcanic eruption. This page, clockwise from the top: A view from Volcan Chico, Sierra Negra, on Isabela Island; the shore of South Plaza Island; a tornito or spatter "oven" on Santiago (James Island). Opposite page: Punta Espinosa, Fernandina Island. Overleaf: Santiago (James Island).

the great volcano on Fernandina, and had no fonder memory than sitting on Angermeyer's veranda, "surrounded on all sides by prying marine iguanas. They sat down at my feet and hissed as they begged for food like young dachshunds."

If we'd had time to explore the island, we could have found on Santa Cruz a sampling of all the principal Galápagoan ecosystems. There are actually seven fairly distinct vegetation types. We were already familiar with the first two—the sea-level littoral zone and the arid zone with its sentinel-like stands of *Opuntia* tree-cactus. Gaining altitude, you pass through a transitional zone into the evergreen *Scalesia* forest (the limit of our explorations) where the thicket-like undergrowth can make for difficult going. The *Scalesia* group is unique to the Galápagos, the trees being anywhere from 20 to 40 feet high and fairly ragged in appearance, since the dead leaves are not shed but continue to hang down beneath the living green foilage. Looking upward from a sharp curve in the road, we imagined we could just get a hint of the higher-altitude zones: the liverwort-draped "brown" zone, which started at the upper limit of the *Scalesia* forest, only to disappear in turn beneath the dense canopy of the *Miconia* forest, and finally, at the highest elevations, a pampas-like region—almost never seen by tourists—with a cover of sedges, ferns and grasses.

Darwin Research Station, Academy Bay, about ten minutes' hike from Puerto Ayora. We knock at the gate and learn we're an hour early. The director lets us in anyway, and we get a quick tour of the tortoise corrals, a short lecture—and an appeal for funds.

Charles Darwin Research Station is supposed to be the only place where tourists can approach and even touch the tortoises. Here, the endan-

gered species of the islands are brought to mate and to have their eggs incubated and the young reared at the Station's rearing center until able to fend for themselves. Tortoises of the more arid islands of Española and Pinzón are present, distinguished by a saddle-backed carapace; for the tortoises of the more humid and arable island of Santa Cruz, this modification (which allows them to reach higher for food) was not necessary, as food is within easy reach. Although these tortoises are eventually returned to their native islands, they may still have to fend against the predations of domesticated animals gone feral.

The Galápagos archipelago is home to diverse life underwater, as well as on land. This page, counter-clockwise from the top: Scalloped hammerhead sharks (Sphyrna lewini); a diver with a whale shark (Rhincodon typus); a "school" of hammerhead sharks; a scalloped hammerhead shark seen close-up. Opposite page: The whale shark (top) is the world's largest fish; scalloped hammerheads sharks (bottom) are often found swimming in groups. Overleaf, page left: Slipper lobster (top); Fasciolura, Academy Wall, Santa Cruz Island. Overleaf, page right: A king or passer angel (top); grouper (bottom).

Meeting the tortoises is an awesome experience. With their ponderous movements, great wrinkled necks, the ancient-looking beaks and dark-ringed, tearing eyes, these antediluvian beasts arouse an unaccountable sense of awe and pity. They look so ancient, you could imagine that the individual in front of you had personally witnessed the predations of the buccaneers and whalers, watched his fellows carried off by the tens of thousands.

It was the tortoises that first alerted Darwin to the fact that the various islands within the archipelago were inhabited by different sets of beings. As he tells us, "My attention was first called to this fact by the Vice-Governor, Mr. Lawson, declaring that the tortoises differed from the dif-

ferent islands, and that he could with certainty tell from which island any one was brought." Until then, Darwin continues, "I never dreamed that islands, about fifty or sixty miles apart, and most of them in sight of each other, formed of precisely the same rocks, placed under a quite similar climate, rising to a nearly equal height, would have been differently tenanted." It was this observation, of course, that would become

natural habitat. Once above 500 feet or so, we were in damp, spicy-smelling woods, with moss-hung branches and thickets of water-jeweled, impenetrable undergrowth. Vermillion flycatchers, which at home are so timid as to be invisible, approach cheekily to within a few feet from us. Other than that, it seems almost like a "normal" North American-style environment—until the ground suddenly drops away at your feet and you're looking down into a deep caldera-type crater a mile or

more across.

Camped at the lip of one of these calderas we found a group of Belgian biologists, in the Galápagos to study land snails. (Luckily, none of them were sleepwalkers.) They were breaking camp that day, and were somewhat heavy-hearted about it. Like other scientists we would meet in or away from the islands, they made it clear that

the fundamental starting point of his evolutionary theory.

The Research Station maintains two tortoise reserves in the humid zone, fifteen or so miles from the town. Our package tour, alas, left little time for excursions ashore, and missing the reserves was one of those frustrations we had to endure for the sake of visiting as many islands as possible. As chance would have it, we managed to have our cake and eat it, too.

A dozen or so of us pile into a hired truck and follow a red dirt road that winds north into the highlands; our plan is to see some tortoises in their

This page, clockwise from the top left: Hydroids; a cardinal hawkfish on gorgonian, which is a horn-like coral; grouper; pufferfish (Diodon holocanthus). Opposite page: Pufferfish (top); cardinal hawkfish (bottom). Hawkfishes are known for their immobility— hardly ever moving.

the opportunity to do field research in the Galápagos was the thrill of their lives.

Heading back down, we make a detour. A ten-year-old local girl with a sweet serious face and a pink transistor radio has offered to guide us to some galápagos that live near her home. We follow her to a sloping meadow where three tortoises are grazing peacefully. Tortoises in the wild! Success!

Back on the *Iguana*, there was a bit of an argument over our unscheduled ramble. The naturalists were annoyed because the outing was

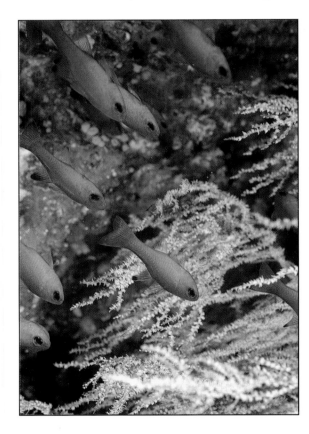

unauthorized and dangerous as well as unplanned. (It also turned out that there had been other trouble as well: another small group had wandered off and got lost, missed the *panga* back to the ship, and had to be ferried "home" by the Darwin Station's launch—while a couple of tourists in yet another group had fainted from the heat.) On the other hand, it was our only chance to visit the highlands, so from our viewpoint it was worth a bit of risk. Easy to see their point of view, though. Everything we saw seemed to emphasize the fragility of the islands' ecology; it

This page, clockwise from the top right: Lobster; a fanged blenny; sea urchin; cardinal fish, which is usually found in shallow water. Opposite page: Spineless sea urchin (top); Tabastrea or cup corals (bottom).

was hard to blame those in charge for wanting to control the tourists, who were becoming dramatically more numerous each year.

Sadly, the tortoises of Santa Cruz, as well as all the islands, are severely endangered. While human violence has more or less ceased, the tortoises still suffer terribly from the depredations of introduced animals, particularly wild pigs and dogs. On Santa Cruz, the answer so far has been to protect the young with walled enclosures. And hunt the pigs. On Floreana, donkeys, rats, dogs and cats have wiped out the aboriginal tortoise population, as well as the doves and mockers. On Isabela the problem is cattle and dogs. Some Isabela tortoises are protected by living within the volcanic craters. On Santiago (James) Island, goats are the main problem. With an area of 225 square miles, the island had a goat population of 100 to 150 thousand—down from a high of over a half-million before the control pro-

This page, top: A surgeon fish feeds. Surgeonfishes are so called because of the "blades" in either side of the fish, just in front of the tail. Bottom: A school of jacks, big and amber varieties. Jacks are excellent gamefishes, good-tasting but hard to catch. Opposite page: A lizard fish may spend its time laying in wait for prey (top); soap fish (bottom).

gram began—and they ate virtually all the vegetation. On tiny Pinta (Abingdon Island), 34,000 goats had been killed by the start of the 1980s, but the 200 or so that remained were a persistent threat to the native wildlife.

South Plaza Island. The water was fairly rough, but we managed to make a dry landing on a low concrete jetty. A largish sea lion bull apparently regards the jetty as his territory, and he lunged at Philippe, one of our naturalist guides, who escaped a nasty bite only by fancy footwork that would have done Charlie Chaplin proud. A comic sight—but this same bull injured another guide fairly seriously a week and a half ago.

If you could visit just one island, you might want it to be gem-like South Plaza. Tiny and delightful, it offers an astonishing diversity literally at arm's length: a sea lion harem on the beach, complete with nursing pups; and land iguanas browsing like ruminative dinosaurs at the foot of an *Opuntia* grove. The cliffs, lit by the slanting afternoon sun, were densely crowded with graceful swallowtail gulls, boobies (and their enemies the frigates), petrels, shearwaters, and a handful of red-billed tropicbirds. The abrupt tropical dusk descended as we waited for the tenders, casting the blunt *Opuntia* tree-cacti into eerie silhouette, the dark silence broken only by the plash of waves and soft cries of sea lion mothers and pups.

Santiago (James) Island. I slept on the ship's top deck and woke early as we cruised into Buccaneer Cove, South James Bay. High cliffs to port, then wet landing at low tide, with blue-foots on rocks with pelicans. We walked from there over the lava beach and a series of eerie natural bridges, formed by bubbles in the cooling rock.

The green sea turtle (Chelonia mydas) swims gracefully in its element. This page, counter-clockwise from the top: Green sea turtle takes off as a diver approaches; green sea turtle rests on the ocean floor; green sea turtle swimming near Santa Fé Island. Opposite page: green sea turtle swimming near the ocean bottom (top); turtle silhouetted amid a school of fish (bottom).

Buccaneer Cove, which at one time had one of the few fresh springs in the islands (since dried up), was a favorite anchorage for English pirates in the 17th and 18th centuries.

Darwin spent a week on this island, part of the time with a party of Spaniards who had come over from Charles (Santa Maria) Island to dry fish and to obtain and salt tortoise meat. He also went with them in their whale-boat to a *salina*—a crater where a layer of crystalized white salt lay beneath three or four inches of water. "The lake is quite circular," he reported, "and is fringed with a border of bright green succulent plants; the almost precipitous walls of the crater are clothed with wood, so that the scene was altogether both picturesque and curious. A few years since, the sailors belonging to a sealing-vessel murdered their captain in this quiet spot; and we saw his skull lying among the bushes."

From the beach we follow a sandy path to the "seal grotto," stepping carefully to avoid the lava lizards—very numerous. (One of them carried a dead finch chick

This page, clockwise from the top left: A spotted eagle ray; a densely quartered school of bonito; manta ray and jacks silhouetted against the surface; a pair of remoras fastened into the head of this manta ray. Opposite page: Pacific Manta ray (Manta hamiltoni), top; wrasse mating (bottom). The size of a species of wrasse may vary anywhere from three inches to ten feet.

in its jaws.) The grotto is ashy-black lava washed by the surf. We don snorkels and face masks and gingerly let ourselves down into a deep cleft in the rock. It's like diving into the neck of a brilliant turquoise bottle, spangled with brilliantly colored fish and sea urchins. After a minute or two the fur seals join us, singly and in groups of four or five.

After all we'd read and heard about the Galápagos animals' extraordinary lack of fear, were still unprepared for the delightful experience of diving with the fur seals. They played with each other and with us, scratching at themselves with a flipper, spiraling—dancing?—together in a floating ballet, lithe, silken, unspeakably winsome and somehow *sexy* with their enormous, impassive dark eyes. They have no objection if you reach out and stroke them, and are apt to return the favor. The naturalist Michael Jackson reports, "I have had my fins and regulator tubes pulled by inquisitive sea lions on many occasions." Their calm acceptance of your presence seems to put you on a new and companionable footing with nature—exhilarating and at the same time somewhat humbling.

Wet landing at long, shallow Espumilla Beach, on the west side of Santiago. A small flock of oystercatchers, with comically upcurved orange bills, were chasing the

scrub, to get a close-up view of a Galápagos hawk mother on her nest. Soon we're going slower, working through lichen-draped palo santo forest (many audacious mockers, warbler finches, black finches, Galápagos doves) and then up a steep escarpment. Broken lava covered with growth—very rough going. Finally reach cliff over hawk's tree, tired, sweaty, cut in places.

The nest was two or three feet across, with a

As we began our descent, a loud clattering further uphill in the woods alerted us to a family of feral goats. Their appearance was a surprise. We had thought of them only in their role as ecological villains—"hoofed locusts," to use John Muir's phrase. They may have indeed been pests suitable only for extermination, but they were also magnificent, shaggy-coated creatures with bold brown and black markings, whose curved

retreating waves in neat swift lines. We hike through mangrove area and continue for about a half-mile past the flamingo lagoon. No flamingos, but hordes of pintails, stilts, flycatchers, and hermit crabs. The stream bank is virtually carpeted with tiny fiddler crabs, maybe an inch long, dancing over the mud, each waving a (relatively) enormous pink claw in the air.

Several species of mangrove occur in the Galápagos, easily recognized by their green glossy leaves and the interlocking prop roots that look like a tangle of stilts. They are the pioneer plants of the beaches and lagoons, their adventitious roots, which rapidly spread underground, helping to stabilize the shore and provide a sort of natural catch-basin in which other plant and animal species thrive.

We follow a path up through what begins as easy

dark brown female and two chicks. We moved cautiously, partly from prudence—the mother, with her impressive yellow talons, looked eminently capable of defending her domain. But we are also in awe: With only about 200 pairs left in the wild, this bird was one of the rarest on earth.

This page, clockwise from the top left: A vermilion flycatcher (Pyrocephalus rubinus), Santa Cruz Island; a yellow warbler (Dendroica petechia); a Galápagos flycatcher, Santiago (James Island); an American oystercatcher (Haematopus palliatus), Santiago (James Island). Opposite page: Ruddy turnstones, Punta Espinosa, Fernandina Island (top); a swallow-tailed gull (Creagus furcatus), (bottom).

horns reached nearly two feet in length.

A group of dolphins materialize at our bows and give us a show. They keep pace with the Iguana effortlessly (20 knots or so) & elegantly—& hardly seem to move a muscle. They'll leap from the water, roll past and over one another, sometimes shooting off at right angles to chat with a friend or attend to some private business, then return at torpedo speed and pace the boat for awhile. Eventually they seem to tire of our cheers(or possibly of the Iguana's laborious chugging) and wander off.

"I don't suppose there is any more inspiring

sight than a school of dolphins leaping round a ship," Beebe wrote. "They are so unmistakably and thoroughly enjoying themselves, in their effortless rush and curving, easy leaps, that no one could help feeling that almost affectionate sympathy which is inspired by watching anything done superlatively well by someone who has tremendous fun in doing it."

Tagus Cove, Isabela Island. The cove is an elongated bay formed when the sea ate its way through the southern wall of a tuff cone. We land at a dry river bed. The whalers called this Port Rendezvous, and some have left their mark on the rocks, e.g., GENIE 1846. Also nearby is the grave of an American sailor, Andy Marino, who drowned here in 1952.

Sailors' graves used to be a fairly common sight on the islands. For many years a wooden cross on James marked the grave of Midshipman John S. Cowan with the words, "Here, in 1813, fell in a daybreak duel, a Lieutenant of the U.S. frigate Essex, aged twenty-one; attaining his majority in death." Andy Marino's grave prompted one of the guides to tell us the macabre tale of a scientist who drowned on an expedition some years ago. Officials refused to allow the body

The diversity of wild-life—especially birds—in the Galápagos archipelago caught Darwin's attention. This page, clockwise from the top right: A land iguana, (Conolophus subcristatus) on South Plaza Island; a yellow warbler (Dendroica petechia) in the sesuvium on South Plaza Island; a cactus finch (Geospiza scandens) feeding on Opuntia flowers, Santa Fé Island; mockingbird nesting in Opuntia, Santiago (James Island). Opposite page: Cactus groundfinch, its beak speckled with pollen. Overleaf: Bartolomé Island.

out of the country. Not wanting him buried in a strange land, his friends ingeniously cut their late colleague in parts and sent him home as cargo. Most deaths here are by drowning, but on Santa Cruz the drivers of what were then the only two cars on the island had been killed in a head-on collision.

We separate into two groups. Half of us will hike up the edge of a cinder cone under brutal sun, the others will cruise the bay in the ship's tenders. Our group (the first ashore) hikes to a high prominence where we could see across Isabela to the open water beyond, massive lava fields covering most of the terrain below.

The volcano just north of Tagus Cove has a salt lake at the bottom of the crater. This was the one visited by Darwin when the *Beagle* was anchored in Tagus Cove on September 29, 1835.

We cruise by the cliffs for an hour. Graffiti mar the hills and cliffs, but incredible close-up views of noddy terns, blue-foots, penguins, pelicans, lava flows, red lava crabs. Flightless cormorants, like their mainland cousins, stand on shore and comically hold out their straggly wings to "dry." Evolution has trimmed their wing feathers, but they still retain the instinctive behavior pattern that was a part of the flier's life.

Man's coming has brought an unexpected threat to the Galápagos' cormorants: they often are trapped and die in lobster traps. We learned of another hazard to cormorants—gluttonous overeating—when we dropped anchor at lunchtime. Fernando, the *Iguana's* first mate, fed what he called kitchen scraps—actually vast quantities of raw meat—to a flightless cormorant that he referred to as *mi amigo Paco*. It drove the naturalists crazy to see the wildlife being handled like performing circus animals, and brought to the surface an always-simmering conflict between naturalists and residents. Many old-time settlers regard the scientists' warnings against handling the native fauna as so much old-maidish fussing; they regard the tame animals basically as pets. And some of them have apparently raised strenuous objections to the goat extermination program, since it deprives them of what they consider an important "natural" food source.

Crossing a deep channel (almost 900 fathoms, according to the map), we land at Punta Espinoza on Fernandina Island and walk uphill over horrific, crevasse-strewn lava formations. A brutal, desolate vista, dominated by the profile of Fernandina's distant, smoldering caldera.

This was the scene that so impressed Mel-

The Galápagos archipelago is home to colonies of the Greater Flamingo (Phoenicopterus ruber ruber), which can be found on many of its islands. This page, clockwise from the top: Greater flamingo on Rábida (Jervis Island); a flock of greater flamingoes wading on the shore of Rábida; a greater flamingo wades in the waters off Floreana. Opposite page: Close-up of the greater flamingo.

ville and all those parched early explorers: the sun and heat merciless, the stone underfoot like broken steel. Even knowing that our ship was nearby with dinner and cold beer waiting, the sense of desolation, of immense earth forces at work—of our own insignificance in this merciless landscape—was ultimately oppressive. The novelist Kurt Vonnegut set one of his latest books in the Galápagos, and it was a good choice. In this blasted, hellish, slag-heap of a landscape, the abstract notion of extinction suddenly becomes personal and extremely vivid.

Where the rock meets the sea, in contrast, we find lush mangrove stands alive with shore birds & pelican nests. Flightless cormorants also nest here, and a large colony of marine iguanas cover a sizable rock just off the northernmost point of land.

"It is a hideous-looking creature," Darwin wrote of the marine iguana, "of a dirty black colour, stupid, and sluggish in its movements." He noticed that when frightened, they would

Lava formations give the Galápagos its distinctive terrain. This page, clockwise from the top: Pahoehoe-type formation on Santiago (James Island); a pyroclastic cone, Bartolomé Island; a cinder cone on the west flank of Volcan Alcedo, on Isabela Island. Opposite page:

The combinations of pounding surf and lava flow make for the Galápagos' very jagged coastline. Overleaf: Not all of the Galápagos is barren, as this lush forest attests.

not enter the water, though they swam with "perfect ease and quickness." "I threw one several times as far as I could, into a deep pool left by the retiring tide; but invariably it returned in a direct line to the spot where I stood." His explanation of this seeming stupidity was simply: the iguana had nothing to fear on shore (until Darwin came) whereas at sea it could easily become a meal for a shark. "Hence, probably, urged by a fixed and hereditary instinct that the shore is its place of safety, whatever the emergency may be, it there takes refuge."

The pools and lagoons are thick with sea lion mothers and nursing pups—an incongruously tender vignette in this savage landscape. Heading back to the jetty, we stop to watch two mother sea lions wrangle for a spot in the path; once the winner was comfortably settled, a waiting lava lizard darted forward to pick the flies off her haunches.

Sea lions are distinctly more territorial than the gentler fur seals, but the territoriality (except among the harem-ruling males) is limited to their own kind. Beebe described an unexpected en-

counter with a sea lion pup while exploring a tidal pool: "He looked at me with all his soul, and forthwith broke into a loud, raucous wail. A deep roar sounded from the other side of a barrier of huge boulders, and instantly there appeared, swiftly swimming and banking on the turn, a mother sea lion and two more infants. She saw me at once and her fear died so instantly that it was not wholly complimentary. She might have explained it, 'That thing, whatever it is, is not a shark, so it's all right!' "

The dolphins are back for a night show, beaks and fins outlined in phosphorescent plankton as they frolic in the greenly glowing wake.

This magical spectacle—each speeding dolphin seemed to be illuminated by its own faint greenish spotlight—had a mundane explanation: the tiny copepods and crustaceans that make up the oceanic plankton, like many deep-sea life forms, are bioluminescent. The jostling they get as the dolphins move starts a biochemical reaction that causes each to give off a faint spark of light.

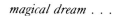

Darwin studied this, and ascribed the luminescence of the southern sea simply to "torn and irregular particles of gelatinous matter near the surface." Beebe, the scientist-poet, took unending joy in hanging over the bow at night: "The ship ploughs a deep furrow through miles of star dust—phosphorescence which will fill the last imaginative human being as full of wonder and awe as it did the first who ever ventured out to sea."

When their encore performance is done, the dolphins depart as abruptly as they had the day before. Suddenly we realize that tomorrow is our last full day in the islands, and a mournful farewell depression seems to settle over the company—or is it just me?—as though we know we will soon be forced to wake from a magical dream . . .

By this time the *Iguana* had become a sort of home to us, more solid than land. We even had our sea legs: aboard ship we seemed to be motionless, steady; standing up ashore, we sometimes seemed to have a sensation of swaying. As though to assuage our melancholy, the last day was arranged to include *three* landfalls.

Dry landing on north shore of tiny Bartolomé Island, near a sunken volcanic cone that swarms with the tiny Galápagos penguins.

We never got used to the sight of penguins at the Equator, but in fact they find the cool, nutrient-rich waters of the Galápagos quite hospitable. The Galápagos species is small and drab compared to its Antarctic cousins, and on shore has been known to zip along speedily on all fours, using the fins as "forelegs." Despite their clownish appearance, Darwin found these birds to have firmness of character: "Having placed myself between a penguin . . . and the water, I was much amused by watching its habits. It was a brave bird; and till reaching the sea, it regularly fought and drove me backwards. Nothing less than heavy blows would have stopped him: every inch he gained he firmly kept, stand-

These pages: The flightless cormorant (Nannopterum harrisi) is a native of the Galápagos. Although it is the largest of cormorants, its wings are too small for it to fly. It can be found on many of the islands, including Fernandina, Isabela, and Sante Fé Islands. Overleaf, page left: A flightless cormorant with a Sally Lightfoot crab (Grapsus grapsus), Punta Espinosa, Fernandina Island. Overleaf, page right: Flightless cormorants change over at their nest, Isabela Island.

the mountains and textures were formed violently and abruptly, and nature has done nothing to soften their original outlines. Captain Benjamin Morrell of the sealing ship *Tartar* was becalmed about ten miles off Fernandina during a violent eruption in 1825, and his journal gives a vivid picture of what it's like to be in the neighborhood when such a landscape is taking form. Two hours after the fireworks began, a river of melted lava a quarter of a mile wide began to rush seaward, branching as it went. "The demon of fire seemed rushing to the embraces of Neptune," Morrell wrote, "and dreadful indeed was the uproar occasioned by their meeting. The ocean boiled and roared and bellowed, as if a civil war had broken out in the Tartarean gulf." The ocean temperature rose to 105 degrees, the air to 123 degrees; the melted pitch was running from the *Tartar's* seams and the tar dropping from her rigging before a merciful breeze sprang up to carry them safely away.

Sullivan Bay is still almost sterile after eighty-plus years, except for colonies of *Brachycereus* cactus and *Mollugo*, but it offers impressive specimens of the lava type known by the Hawaiian name, *pahoehoe*. The rapid cooling of the still-

ing close before me erect and determined.''

Our path wanders up the island's eastern slopes, a moonscape of desolate lava tubes, pumice, and cinder "spatter cones" formed by brief eruptions, with a 390-foot-high cinder cone roughly in the center, which we climb. From the upper slope we can barely make out Pinta and Marchena, the larger of the northern islands, on the far side of the equator.

Pinta is known for its awesome coastal cliffs, Marchena for its volcanic cones and lava flows (which nearly obscure the original volcanic summit) and the fumaroles, smaller cavities that still pour forth hot gases. Both are well off the usual visitor's route. Beyond them, another sixty miles or so past the northern horizon, tiny Culpepper and Wenman islands, the tops of two undersea volcanoes, thrust forbidding cliffs hundreds of feet above the sea. A few intrepid explorers have landed on Wenman, the larger, but no one at all had set foot on Culpepper until a helicopter landed there in 1964. This magnificent isolation is no drawback to winged visitors, who make their nests in great numbers on both islands, especially Culpepper: great frigatebirds, boobies (masked and red-footed), swallowtailed gulls, red-billed tropicbirds and sooty terns, which have established their only Galápagos nesting ground under Culpepper's *croton* bushes. Wenman also harbors a unique finch species, the sharp-billed ("blood-eating") ground finch.

Wet landing at Sullivan Beach on Bartolomé, an enclosed crescent-shaped beach fringed by mangrove swamp. Snorkeling, frolicking in water. Penguins on shore, reef fish below, pelicans & boobies in air, Pinnacle Rock towering above to the west. To the west, the entire visible coast of nearby Santiago, from Sullivan Bay south and on up the island's eastern slopes, consists of a huge flow of black basaltic lava—formed by a great eruption in 1897 and still largely barren.

Most of us are used to what might be called a "gradualist" geology, or a landscape that has been slowly built, uplifted and eroded over the eons. In the "catastrophist" landscape of the Galápagos,

By the shore it seems that Sally Lightfoot crabs (Grapsus grapsus) can be found everywhere. This page, top to bottom: Sally Lightfoots in surf, Sombrero China; as seen here, Sally Lightfoots are bright against the lava rocks; a Sally Lightfoot at a burrow in a rock-crevice. Opposite page: Lightfoots crowd the shores at Punto Egas, Santiago (James Island), top; Lightfoots in the surf at Point Tortuga. Overleaf: Punto Suares, Española (Hood Island).

flowing lava gave rise to a crust that twisted and buckled while still plastic and ultimately hardened into all sorts of fantastic shapes. Many seem weirdly organic: twisted, ropy folds, like blackened animal innards; finger-like protrusions known locally as "lava toes"; other shapes like hornets' nests, bulging sacs, or a monstrous, mineralized rhinoceros hide.

North Seymour Island. The landing was supposed to be "dry," but the old dock had collapsed some time back and the water was extremely rough. One of our pilots fell in, and was pulled out just before getting a leg crushed. Path through the island was level, led through booby colony—blue-foots courting, honking, whistling, sky-pointing, brooding—to a large, noisy colony of magnificent frigate birds.

Both of the Galápagos frigatebird species, the magnificent frigatebird (*Fregata magnificens*) and the great frigatebird (*F. minor*), build untidy, platform-like nests of interlaced twigs—almost invariably using material stolen from a booby or another frigate. For three or four weeks in the breeding season, the male frigate's gular (throat) pouch turns from pink to bright scarlet, and can be inflated like a balloon. It serves the same purpose as the peacock's tail—a flamboyant accessory for courtship display. When it is fully expanded, to about the size of a soccer ball, he positions himself on a suitable roost, four-inch beak pointed skyward.

The appearance of a female overhead prompts

him to a spectacular display: he spreads his glossy wings and trembles them violently, calls loudly in a high, ululating falsetto, and throws his head back and wags his beak from side to side to display his inflated throat sac in its full splendor. Eventually (if he is fortunate) a female will descend for a closer look, and if all goes well, she will finally join in his head-wagging, and the mutual display will continue for several hours. Courtship among the great frigates is a sensuous-looking affair. The male, wings still extended, sometimes seems to embrace the female, while the incipient partners pass their heads and bills repeatedly across one another's neck.

On the beach path back, we have eighteen or so lazy sea lions for company; also a scattering of nearly jet-black marine iguanas, a race endemic to this island. Plenty of swooping, graceful swallowtail gulls, too, with one chick and one juvenile in nests close to the landing place.

Great colonies of the great frigatebird (Fregata minor) are to be found in the Galápagos archipelago. One of world's great fliers, the frigatebird's wingspan and its long forked tail allow it great maneuverabilty. This page, clockwise from the top: A flock of male and female great frigatebirds; a male great frigatebird flies with his throat pouch inflated; a frigatebird carries nesting materials. Center: Immature great frigatebirds chase each other over food, Tower Island (top); a frigatebird diving for food (bottom).

This page, clockwise from the top: Great frigatebirds (Fregata minor) in flight; a female great frigatebird and her chick; a female and chick, Tower Island. Opposite page: A mature male frigatebird inflates his pouch (top) to indicate his readiness to mate; an immature frigatebird by its nest on Tower Island (bottom). Overleaf: Frigatebirds at sunset.

It seemed fitting to end our last island visit in the company of the endemic swallow-tailed gull, *Creagrus furcatus*, which had been a sort of visual grace note in many of our previous outings. A swallowtail in breeding plumage is easily the most beautiful of all Galápagos creatures: a smallish, slender bird with dramatically shaded gray-and-white plumage, black head and wingtips, pink feet and scarlet eye-ring and (in flight) forked white tail. They prefer to nest on cliffs, but also do well on lava, sand or—as at North Seymour—

on shingle beaches. Unusual among gull species, the swallowtail is a nocturnal feeder. Its large, dark-adapted eyes help in finding and catching squid and small fish near the surface of the sea. Adults leave the nest at dusk, returning several times during the night to feed their young.

Back aboard the *Iguana* that night, Jim and Philippe, the chief guides, burst into the ship's saloon, one dressed as King Neptune, the other as a bloodthirsty pirate chieftain with sword and eye-patch. They angrily accused us of invading

This page, clockwise from the top right: A great frigatebird male (Fregata minor) in full mating display, Tower Island; a frigatebird at nest; immature great frigatebirds (left and right). Opposite page: Great frigatebird chick on Tower Island (top); Mated great frigatebirds. Overleaf, page left: Immature magnificent frigatebird (Fregata magnificens). Opposite page: Male great frigatebird (top); frigatebird with young (bottom).

what by now is the usual complement of cormorants, boobies, pelicans, ground finches, sea lions and frigates.

Looking back as our twin-engined plane laboriously gained altitude for the two-and-a-half-hour flight to Guayaquil, we realized for the first time how tiny these islands are—how tiny and how vulnerable. Baltra is, or should be, an object lesson: the native fauna was not just decimated in World War II; it was *exterminated,* and the effects are still clear. One of the scientists with our group saw lava lizards on our walk to the airport; nothing more. I saw only grasshoppers.

We realized that we'd been looking at a vanishing heritage. After a few days, we had become accustomed to the sight of the marine iguanas, the flightless cormorants, or the Darwin's finches and become somewhat blasé about them. Their abundance here made us forget momentarily that they are the only ones of their kind, outside of a few specimens in zoos. Some other species, like the waved albatross, live elsewhere but breed here and nowhere else in the world; if

their territory by daring to cross the equator, and ended by viciously assaulting all of the passengers with pies in the face. Every voyager's first crossing of the equator is supposed to be marked with some such ceremony (usually involving some sort of total immersion) and we had crossed *four* times by then, so we figured we were getting off easy. When we had wiped or licked ourselves

off, each of us received a handsome certificate attesting to our new status as shellbacks.

Spent last night moored off Baltra (South Seymour); offloaded early, and most of us walked the two miles to the airfield. A flat, gray-brown island: concrete wharf, corrugated metal sheds, feces and toilet paper floating in the water—an incongruous setting for

anything were to disrupt that, the consequences would be permanent.

I recalled the words of the British ornithologist Bryan Nelson, written over twenty years ago. "The Galápagos Islands mean primal, undisturbed paradises," Nelson wrote, "where birds treat man with the same fearlessness they bestow on cattle. The Galápagos have always had,

and it is fervently to be hoped will always have, this aura of magic, of unreality. Crazy things happen there and it is still very possible to feel a strong emotional kinship with animals because of their trust and curiosity."

I thought about that as the islands vanished into the clouds beneath us. I hoped we would continue to feel that kinship—and to deserve that trust.

This page, clockwise from the top: A cutleaf daisy (Leocarpus pinnatifidus), Floreana Island; a sea anemone, underwater at Tagus Cove, Isabela Island; a passionfruit (Passiflora foetida galapagoensis), Santa Cruz Island; a passionflower, Santa Cruz Island. Opposite page: a jasminocereus flower, Santa Cruz Island. Overleaf, page left: This guano-stained rock face indicates that the cliff is a rookery. Overleaf, page right: Lava tube at Bella Vista on Santa Cruz Island (top); Punta Vicente Roca on Isabela Island.

·◇·◇·

"NOT AS A PREDATOR"

In the equatorial sun, the jagged lava underfoot was like hot, broken iron. The hunter paused, eased the rifle off his shoulder and mopped his face and neck. Below, the steep side of the volcano gradually leveled down and out to a broad bay and a calm, island-dotted sea. Only the footsteps of his five companions broke the

noon silence. Then a slight movement ahead, distinct from the heat shimmer dancing above the rocks, caught his attention. With a single, almost casual movement he raised the weapon, aimed and fired, twice, just as the wild goat began to wheel away. The first .22 slug stopped the animal; the second dropped it. That made sixteen since dawn, around fifty for the group.

To the already numerous ironies of life in the Galápagos Islands, add this: for life to continue there, it must be preceded by slaughter. This scene or one much like it has already been repeated hundreds of thousands of times throughout the archipelago and will be repeated hundreds of thousands more. The weapons may be bullets, traps or poison; the quarry may be dogs or cats, goats, rats, pigs, or wild burros. The death of these aliens is the necessary prelude to the Galápagos' future. This in turn is part of the larger irony: this rugged, forbidding landscape, where a lone human would quickly perish

without outside help, is itself in urgent need of our protection.

In the nineteenth century, the greatest threat to the Galápagos wildlife seemed to be direct human predation. The tortoises were the most conspicuous victims (though iguanas, fur seals, boobies, doves and other birds were also killed). Captain Porter of the frigate *Essex* described a typical round-up *circa* 1813: "We began to lay in our stock of tortoises, the grand object for which every vessel anchors at the Galápagos Islands. Four boats were dispatched every morning for this purpose and returned at night, bringing with them from twenty to thirty each, averaging about sixty pounds. In four days, we had as many on board as would weigh about fourteen tons, which was as much as we could conveniently stow." Whaling ships visiting the Galápagos, Porter added, generally took two or three hundred tortoises on board per visit.

It is no surprise, then, to learn that three of

the fourteen tortoise subspecies that once flourished on the archipelago are now extinct, and a fourth, which lived on Pinta, is represented by a single male, now a permanent resident at the Darwin Station. The surprise is that the damage wasn't worse. Other animals hunted by man—land iguanas and boobies—have also fared badly, but except for some strains of the Galápagos rice rat, populations have been decimated but not extinguished. Luckily for posterity, the land areas

of the Galápagos have been too impoverished and uninviting to make a very tempting target for exploitation.

The plunder of undersea resources—whales, fur seals and the commercial fishery species—has been more enthusiastic, which may be one reason the waters of the archipelago have not, until very recently, had any sort of formal protection. Black coral is a favorite target. This variety of precious coral, dense and beautiful as black ivory,

grows abundantly in some of the deeper Galápagos waters, and was used by local artisans who made jewelry and crafts items—figures of whales, penguins, sea lions—for the tourist trade. Naturalist-photographer James Cribb spent several years recently exploring and photographing the archipelago's underwater fauna. "Occasionally," he wrote in his 1986 book, *Subtidal Galápagos*, "I came across scenes that left my gut in a knot: swatches of submarine landscapes laid bare by

coral hunters; fishing boats at anchor, their decks crowded with rust-stained freezers where thousands of spiny lobsters awaited shipment to the mainland; expanses of empty sea bereft of the all-important food fish that are key links in the food chain of the submarine world. Clearly, humanity has left its unmistakable mark.''

Today the greatest threats on the islands themselves are from animals and plants introduced by man. The eons of isolation have made both the indigenous plants and animals extremely vulnerable to almost any kind of biological invaders. Herbivores browse upon and trample the native vegetation, and new plants can run rampant over existing vegetation. And of course predators can easily catch and overwhelm native species, which lack even the self-protective instinct to flee. Feral dogs, for instance, compete with native species for food and nesting sites, destroy burrows and nests, and devour eggs and young. Dogs have even been reported to kill adult tortoises, by seizing and worrying loose one armor plate, then the next, until the soft flesh is exposed.

Black (or ship) rats established themselves in the mid-1800s, and promptly wiped out five of the seven native species of Galápagos rice rat, the only native terrestrial mammal in the archipelago. The biological effects of introduced invertebrates are less well known, but biologists have found that one species of introduced fire ant has reduced or eliminated many local populations of native ants, spiders and scorpions—and, it might be added, done nothing to make the place more comfortable for human visitors.

Of the major islands, only Fernandina has been spared the effects of introduced animal species. Pinta *had* remained blessedly free of goats until 1959, when a fisherman put two females and one male ashore. Ultimately the three produced more than 40,000 offspring, and their browsing and trampling literally eliminated four species of favorite food plants from the island's lower slopes.

Once introduced to the island environment

(as Darwin might have pointed out) these alien animals and plants are subject to the same laws of adaptation and survival that ruled the endemic species. Under the influence of natural selection, cats become leaner and faster than their domestic forebears. Pigs become lean and boar-like, goats nimble and long-horned, and feral dogs become fierce, long-legged pack hunters. (Photographer Tui De Roy, on a walk with her family, once found herself encircled on a steep lava ridge by a group of eight snarling, fang-baring wild dogs.) These proceedings might, from an Olympian height, be looked upon with some detached interest in the results of this latest evolutionary experiment. However, those on the scene are not disinterested observers; they care passionately about the outcome, and in many cases have committed years and even lifetimes to preserving the islands.

A Partnership for Preservation

The Charles Darwin Research Station at Academy Bay today is a complex of sturdy low white buildings, humming with the activity of fifty scientists, students, conservation workers and other staff. There is little to suggest the complex negotiations and the fierce dedication required to conceive of such a center, impossibly distant

This page, clockwise from the top: The beach at Point Tortuga; blue-footed boobies (Sula nebouxii) *perch on a guano-stained rockface; although flightless cormorants* (Nannopterum harrisi) *are not able to fly, they still go through the motions of drying their wings, like the one pictured here. Opposite page, clockwise from the top left: A short-eared owl* (Asio flammeus) *with its catch; a brown pelican* (Pelecanus occidentalis) *building a nest; a blue-footed booby effects a comical landing on Isabela Island; a blue-footed booby chick.*

(as it seemed in those early years) from the world's scientific centers—let alone to nurture it to its present vigorous health.

There was in fact almost no systematic research in the islands until 1905-06, when scientists from the California Academy of Sciences conducted a major exploration of all the lesser-known islands and remote highlands, and returned with the first major collection since Darwin's. (Academy Bay on Santa Cruz is named for the expedition's schooner *Academy*, which anchored there for an extended time.) Professor Beebe's two expeditions added to his own and the islands' renown and provided the first tantalizing glimpses of the archipelago's rich underwater fauna, and it was another American, ornithologist Harry S. Swarth of the California Academy of Sciences, who conceived the first proposal to extend legal protection to the islands and their wildlife. This was subsequently formulated as an executive decree by Ecuador's President Albelardo Montalvo in 1934, which led, twenty-five tortuous years later, to the establishment of the Station and the Galápagos National Park.

The Station's parent body, the non-profit Charles Darwin Foundation for the Galápagos Islands, is an emphatically international organization, created under the auspices of the government of Ecuador, UNESCO, and the International Union for the Conservation of Nature & Natural

Resources. It is affiliated with the World Wildlife Fund and governed by a 34-person Executive Council, with a Secretary General based in Quito and an Executive Director based at the Smithsonian Institution's National Museum of Natural History in Washington, D.C., and with the Darwin Station as its principal operational arm. Half the Executive Council members are Ecuadorians—scientists, conservationists, business leaders and representatives from the major government agencies and universities—and the balance are eminent persons in similar fields from around the world, including H.R.H. the Duke of Edinburgh and Prince Henri of Luxembourg. ("We're not a very simple organization," comments long-term Executive Director Marsha E. Sitnik.) Its mandate is to provide for the protection of Galápagos wildlife; to support, organize and administer research work at CDRS; to disseminate research findings; and to encourage and aid scientific education, particularly in Ecuador. The Foundation maintains a museum with a collection of Galápagos biological specimens; it awards scholarships to Ecuadorian science students (over four hundred to date) for work at the Station, and conducts research and specialized education, including training of the Park's naturalist-guides.

The Station has hosted several hundred scientific missions to the islands in its first thirty years, and at any given moment about eight to ten scientists and twenty students are doing research there. Their work advances the frontiers of their specialties—systematics, reproductive biol-

The name "booby" is thought to have been derived from the Spanish bobo, *meaning "clown." This page, clockwise from the top: Blue-footed boobies* (Sula nebouxii) *square off in a boundary dispute; blue-footed boobies perched on cliff; blue-footed booby chicks, such as this one, lose their fluff as they grow older. Opposite page: Sunset on Española (Hood Island). Overleaf: Blue-footed boobies line up at the shoreline.*

ogy, ecology and ethology, and so on—and their insights in turn become part of the basis for management and planning decisions by the Station and the Galápagos National Park Service and its parent organization, the National Forestry Directorate (Ministry of Agriculture), which bear the burden of preserving and, if possible, enhancing the wild environment.

Over the years the Station has evolved a unique and highly productive partnership with the

Park Service—nicely illustrated when Miguel Cifuentes, who first came to the islands as one of the Foundation's scholarship students, went on to serve as superintendent of the Galápagos National Park from 1976 through 1986. Station personnel work with the park wardens on a daily basis, and the two institutions prepare their annual plans together each fall, setting technical goals, devising strategies to economize on time, money, and equipment (e.g., by sending scientists and wardens to the same island at same time), and collaborating to ensure that the right questions are asked and the right approaches are taken.

Many studies focus on evolution and animal-

plant interactions. The land iguanas' ancestry, for example, poses something of a puzzle to zoologists; despite resemblances to other large lizards of Central and South America, they actually may be more nearly related to the marine iguanas. Genetic studies can clarify these relationships. Others focus on animal behavior and its evolution, and on ecological relationships among the different species; the simplicity of the Galápagos ecosystems and the harshness of the environment also make the archipelago an ideal laboratory for such studies.

For marine biologists, the Galápagos offer a matchless chance to visit what is still in many respects a virgin underwater environment. Jack Grove, a California-based marine biologist, spent seven years in the Galápagos as a researcher and guide and has compiled the first comprehensive guide to Galápagos fishes. It includes seven "new" fish species, including a type of scorpion fish never seen before except in a shark's stomach and a species of cuskeel (family Ophididae) which has not thus far been described in the scientific literature. "It was exciting and challenging," Grove says, "to be working with fishes that Darwin collected, but for which no one had ever been able to document their breeding habits and seasons, migrations—or, in one case, where no one before had ever seen the fish's colors in life." In these islands once re-named for Columbus, the Age of Discovery is still not quite over.

One of the Darwin Station's most gratifying achievements has been its successful captive-breeding program for the tortoises and land iguanas. To date the Station has hatched more than 1,200 tortoises, representing eight species or sub-

This page, clockwise from the top left: A blue-footed booby (Sula nebouxii) sits in the middle of a perfect guano-ring on North Seymour Island; a juvenile booby tries out its wings; a pair of blue-footed boobies nesting; a blue-footed booby with chick. Opposite page : Blue-footed boobies on cliff (top) and at the shore-line with Sally Lightfoot crabs (Grapsus grapsus), bottom. Overleaf: blue-footed boobies dive for fish at Punta Espinosa, Fernandina Island.

species. They are hand-reared until their shells can resist the attacks of predators and they have a good chance of surviving in the wild; then they are released into their ancestral habitat. The one-thousandth "repatriated" tortoise was freed in 1988, and former Station director Craig MacFarland (now the Charles Darwin Foundation's president) is cautiously optimistic. "The first animals raised in captivity are now reaching adult size and starting to mate themselves, so we're coming full circle," he says. "They're starting to breed, and we'll see now whether they can make it or not. I think we've basically saved them."

The single surviving tortoise from Isla Pinta, affectionately dubbed "Lonesome George," poses a special and intriguing problem in conservation strategy. Naturalists have combed Isla Pinta and searched through zoos the world over to find him a mate, but with no success. What to do next? The Station will probably try two complementary approaches. First, try to store sperm from the animal so as to preserve his pure genetic line (luckily George, at somewhere between 35 and 65 years of age, is still in his vigorous tortoise youth). At the same time, they will try to cross-breed George with females from the race morphologically closest to his own, from Volcan Wolf on Isabela, and then back-cross to purify the line as much as possible. As a backup, there are tentative plans to take 50 or 100 animals from the Volcan Wolf population and put them on

Pinta as breeding stock to repopulate the island. Then if anything goes wrong with the Lonesome George experiment, Pinta will at least have the next-best thing: a population of Pinta-type tortoises being acted on there by natural selection.

An intensive program of breeding and repatriation has also been carried out with three of the most endangered varieties of land iguana. More than 120 individuals now occupy burrows in the soft soil of South Plaza, where they can usually be found browsing at the foot of the *Opuntia* cactus trees—their favorite food source—and more than 250 young iguanas have been settled in their ancestral territories on northwestern Santa Cruz and southeastern Isabela. An interesting experiment will soon be tried on Baltra (South Seymour), which has been a military island since the 1940s and where the endemic land iguanas were wiped out by bored soldiers using them for target practice. It turns out, though, that in the 1930s some visiting scientists, puzzled by the absence of land iguanas on *North* Seymour, put thirty or so Baltra individuals there experimentally. Some of this relict population have now been bred at the Station, and the staff are waiting for a moist year with good plant growth, and they plan to turn several dozen of them loose in their ancestral habitat.

The Station is constantly finding ways to improve its breeding and rearing programs. What

This page, clockwise from the top: Bartolomé Island; gulls in flight over Española (Hood Island); an igneous ledge projecting into the Pacific. Opposite page: Pinnacle Rock on Bartolomé Island.

Darwin called it, "a hideous-looking creature, of a dirty black color, stupid, and sluggish in its movements." Actually the marine iguana (Amblyrhynchus cristatus) is highly adapted to its environment. This page, top: Marine iguana at China Sombrero. Bottom: Marine iguanas blowing salt from their nostrils. Opposite page: Marine iguanas at Punta Espinosa, Fernandina Island (top); contrary evidence to Darwin's statement—a brightly colored marine iguana (bottom).

are the optimum temperature and humidity for incubation? How and how often should the young be fed? On what kind of food? Should animals be kept outside or in closed buildings? There is no end to the questions, but gradually, patiently, the Station staff is working out the best ways to hatch the young of many species and maximize health and weight gain, and sharing their findings with zoos and laboratories around the world.

Closely related to these programs are the Darwin Station's researches in genetics and systematics. For practical purposes, the Station's biologists act on the assumption that each population of tortoises and land iguanas represents a distinct species. The few genetic studies that have been done, using the electrophoresis technique, have tended to confirm the scientists' hunch that the several varieties of lizards, tortoises and so on do in fact constitute "good" (i.e., genetically distinct) species, not just varieties, races, or subspecies. In coming seasons the Foundation hopes to attract researchers from major zoos or private institutions to come in and do advanced work, using the latest "high-tech" genetic identification techniques, such as DNA blueprinting, to determine the actual degree of genetic variability within and among the different populations.

This page, counterclockwise from the top: Marine iguanas (Amblyrhynchus cristatus) *feeding at Punta Egas, Santiago (James Island); marine iguana on Española (Hood Island); marine iguana at the Charles Darwin Research Station (CDRS) on Santa Cruz Island; male marine iguanas at loggerheads, Santa Cruz Islands. Opposite page: A marine iguana with young (top); marine iguanas sunbathing on Fernandina Island (bottom). Overleaf: Marine iguanas on Fernandina Island.*

These questions may sound drearily academic, but the answers can have profound practical implications. Population geneticists, who concern themselves with the quantitative aspects of evolution and survival, look with special concern at two types of numbers: the critical minimum number of individuals needed for a species' survival, and the minimum for a species to have a chance of flourishing over the long term. Below the critical minimum population size, which seems to be around fifty individuals, a species may survive diseases and predators, yet still become extinct within a few generations as a result of random genetic drift, a hereditary process that can cause deleterious or lethal genes to become predominant or "fixed" in a small population.

On the other hand, population genetics suggests that something in the neighborhood of five hundred individuals are needed to assure the species' long-term survival. A population that large is reckoned sturdy enough to survive a period of drought, scarce food supply or an onslaught by parasites or predators, and are expected to adapt healthily to changed environmental

On Santiago (or Hood Island) resides a sub-species of the marine iguana (Amblyrhynchus cristatus), the male of which is particularly brightly colored during the mating season. This page, clockwise from the top left: Lava lizard on top of a marine iguana; a marine iguana at Española (Hood Island); a marine iguana in close-up; a marine iguana at Punta Suarez, Española (Hood Island). Opposite page: a marine iguana clutches a moss-covered rock (top); marine iguanas on the shore at Punta Espinosa, Fernandina Island (bottom). Overleaf, page left: A marine iguana at Punta Espinosa, Fernandina Island. Overleaf, page right: Although the marine iguana, such as these (top and bottom) are aquatic, they spend the majority of their time sunning themselves on rocks at the shoreline.

conditions. Every effort, therefore, is made to get each population up to the five-hundred mark as quickly as possible. Ten years ago, populations of three types of land iguana and four types of tortoise were far below that point, MacFarland explains. "The Hood tortoise population was down to fifteen animals; we got that back up to around three hundred. Pinzón was down to a hundred, and is also back to three hundred, and both are increasing."

Of all research done at the Darwin Station, possibly the least glamorous, yet most important, is about finding ways to control or eliminate alien species. One just-completed project was a program to eliminate black rats from Duncan (Pinzón) Island, the steep, rugged island due west of Santa Cruz, where they had become the worst predators on tortoise eggs and young. After field trials on a smaller island, a very intensive campaign was carried out with more than 35 participants over eighteen days in 1988, using sophisticated, heavy-duty traps and a combination of several kinds of poisons specific to small mammals but not dangerous to the other fauna. The entire 70-square-mile island, consisting mostly of brush-covered, boulder-strewn lava flows, was covered on a grid system; inaccessible coastal

conditioning to pursue agile quarry over jagged lava overgrown with dense shrubbery. As one warden put it, "Predator control here is very, very rough work."

When the goats or other aliens are removed, the native vegetation recovers rapidly, but this can raise new problems. In fact, the ecologists and managers are just beginning to fully understand the dimensions of the complex ecological balancing act involved in establishing a new equilibrium. Many of the aliens keep one another in check, and it's easy to throw the system out of whack.

When park wardens eliminated many of the goats on Floreana, for example, the feral dogs, which had formerly preyed on the goats, began to attack farm poultry. Farmers shot the dogs, and before long the goats were back. In the humid areas of Santiago, browsing by goats eliminates the vegetation that shelters the wild pigs, which in turn control the goat population by eating their young. For the moment, at least, both species are "needed." On Pinta the goats, awful as they were, did at least maintain small open areas amidst the island's heavy vegetation—an ecological function formerly filled by tortoises. With the goats gone, the island is in danger of losing an important complex of more than two dozen shade-intolerant plant species, which require such a dry, open environment. The plan to stock Pinta with tortoises from Volcan Wolf is partly intended to anticipate this problem.

·◇·◇·

These pages: The chief food of the marine iguana (Amblyrhychus cristatus) is seaweed, and the marine iguana is capable of swimming to depths of ten meters or so in order to feed. On shore, however, the marine iguana prefer to bask immobile in the hot, equatorial sun—often in packs. Overleaf, pages left and right: The Galápagos hawk (Buteo galapagoensis).

areas were circled in a rubber dinghy and the bait thrown on shore, to make sure every spot was covered. While the final results are not yet in, the scientists are optimistic. "I don't think anything this big has ever been attempted," MacFarland said afterward. "If we have succeeded, this will be the biggest island—not just in the Galápagos, but anywhere—ever to be cleared of rats, once they were well established."

The primary responsibility for controlling alien species belongs to the Park Service wardens. Of the main islands, only Hood, Fernandina, Rábida, Marchena, Santa Fé, the Plaza Islets, and Tower are free of alien animals; the four inhabited islands and Santiago are all badly infested with feral goats, pigs, burros, rats and other species, though programs are under way on several to control some of these in restricted areas. Pigs, for example, can be shot in the giant tortoises' nesting sites, and the nests themselves can be protected by constructing stone walls. On Pinta, Park Service wardens shot the first 38,000 goats in 1971-75, but repeated sweeps of the island in following years were needed to find and eliminate the rest. The last four or five individuals were rounded up this year using a "Judas goat," a captive animal tagged with a bell and released. The wild goats, being gregarious, collected around her, and the wardens followed the bell (or its modern equivalent, a small radio transmitter) to trap their quarry.

Inevitably, the predator eradication program has its opponents. These include residents, for whom the goats have been an important food source; and animal advocate groups, such as the Fund for Animals. It has also—for somewhat different reasons—caught the attention of meat-packers and sportsmen. Some years back, an enterprising Japanese company tried to negotiate a contract to bring in a refrigerator ship and harvest the goats, but after calculating the ecological risk of putting a sufficient number of hunters in the field and allowing vehicles in to get the carcasses down from the highlands, the Government turned them down. A few overseas hunting groups thought it might be fun to get in on this new field sport, and a number of German hunters actually made it to the islands, but they weren't much help; their subalpine training, alas, gave them neither the expertise nor the physical

Administering Paradise

To visitors looking to find a pristine paradise in the Galápagos, it may come as a shock to learn that the archipelago now has eight substantial towns, on four islands, with a total population of over 10,000. As recently as the mid-1950s, the only inhabited area on Santa Cruz was at Academy Bay, where a few Ecuadorians had joined the few remaining Germans and Norwegians among the clinkers and cactuses. Wreck Bay on San Cristóbal was the other principal town, the archipelago's main port and center of government, with a small Ecuadorian garrison billeted there.

Today Puerto Ayora, with over 4,000 people, is the principal town and economic center, combining the aspects of an unspoiled seaside village with both the features of frontier town and a somewhat gamy tourist resort. The municipal generator provides electricity until midnight or 1:00 AM. There are restaurants, pizzerias, bars, souvenir and T-shirt shops, several small dance halls, and a selection of hotels and *pensiones* (though guests in even the best-kept hostelries are warned against the bite of the fire ants). There is still no telephone contact with the outside world except for the government's official radio communications office, and only one cargo ship a month, so many necessities are in short supply. (There *was* a second supply ship—actually our old friend the M.V. *Iguana*, converted to freighter service—but it struck a reef and sank within sight of the Darwin Station in June 1988.) In other ways the

The Galápagos hawk (Buteo galapagoensis), was once the Islands' fiercest predator; it is now an endangered species. This page, clockwise from the top: An adult Galápagos hawk; an immature hawk with fresh kill, Isabela Island. Opposite page: This Galápagos hawk exhibits the deadly beak and claws of a predatory bird. Overleaf, page left: A green lava heron (Butorides sundevalli) hunting (top); lava heron (Butorides striatus) with catch, Española (Hood Island), bottom. Overleaf, page right: A lava heron on Tower Island.

This page, clockwise from the top: A great blue heron (Ardea herodias), at Punta Espinosa on Fernandina Island; a yellow crowned night heron (Nyetanassa violacea) on Santiago (James Island); a yellow crowned night heron on Tower Island. Opposite page: A great blue heron with prey, Punta Espinosa, Fernandina Island (top); great blue heron at Tortuga Bay, Santa Cruz (bottom). Overleaf, page left: The surf rising from the rocks creates a rainbow (top); Tagus Cove, Isabela Island (bottom). Overleaf, page right: A blowhole at sunrise on Tower Island.

place doesn't seem so isolated anymore. There is now a bus to carry visitors to the highlands for a look at the tortoise reserve, and a high-speed water taxi will now take you to the Plaza Islands (formerly a two-hour trip) in 45 minutes. Busloads of tourists arrive every day from Baltra airport; motorbikes and cars raise dust and decibel levels along the roads, and construction—of houses, hotels, and restaurants—is booming. On other islands, too, new tourist amenities make the place seem less remote. Wreck Bay on San Cristóbal now has several night spots, though the restaurants still close at eight, and on Isabela you can now take a bus nearly to the rim of the seven-mile-diameter caldera of Sierra Negra.

The Galápagos tourism boom began around 1970, when the first package tour brought 60 visitors. Since then the number of visitors has risen dramatically, from 4,500 that year to almost ten times that in 1988. Pressure to capitalize on tourism was inevitable. By the late 1970s there were ominous press reports of developers with visions of "a new Waikiki" on southern Isabela, and of hotel chains with schemes to make the islands "a major tourist mecca." A second airstrip, on San Cristóbal, was added in expectation of this, but so far no such rampant overdevelopment has materialized. There are obvious physical constraints, for one thing. In Academy Bay there are still only two sources of drinking water: rainwater collected off roofs, and a primitive system of plastic pipes that supplies brackish but tolerable water from two volcanic grabens, which form natural catch basins. Still, as California-based geographer Jerry Emory, recently returned from a year's research on Santa Cruz, reported in *National Geographic*, "I discovered tremendous pressures to increase tourism and develop support services, as well as formidable management challenges facing scientists at the Charles Darwin Research Station, the Galápagos National Park Services, and other government agencies."

Surprisingly, the scientists themselves are not particularly worried about tourist expansion. The archipelago actually has only about forty-five "visitable" sites, i.e., places with the right concentrations of interesting plants and animals and scenic beauty to make for a rewarding tourist experience. These account for approximately one-half of one percent of the land, and all are already in use. (For each visitor site, there must be two or three other unvisited sites of high biological quality, where those species can be breeding safely away from possible disturbance.) Tourist management thus becomes a matter of traffic control, regulating the number and timing of visits to any given area, the size of vessels to be permitted, carefully marked trails combined

with high-quality guiding by CDRS-trained guides—and other controls to limit or prevent impact on or abuse of the environment.

The key question, of course, is whether the management capacity exists to handle the increased demand. The existing system is at its limit right now. The Park Service has no patrol boats, for example, and therefore no direct control over inter-island movements. A recent cutback has reduced personnel just at the time when the whole system should be strengthened. But if proper controls, including limitations on overnight stays, can be established and enforced— and it's a very big "if"—it has been suggested that the islands might be able to handle as many as 50,000 to 70,000 visitors a year without significantly overstressing the environment.

A much more insidious threat is posed by two side effects of tourism: human immigration to the islands, and continuing importation of alien

animals and plants. When the national park territories were first laid out, the Government of Ecuador included 97 percent of the land within the park, a figure that is still widely quoted. The reality is, however, incursions by farmers who are clearing the archipelago's land area for graz-

ing, fencing, and harvesting such natural resources as the endemic *mantazarno* (a hardwood that grows in the highlands of some of the larger islands) have reduced that figure to roughly 88 percent.

Within the past few years, the islands' new international cachet has set off a tourism "gold rush" among mainland Ecuadorians. Like every gold rush, it is mostly a cruel illusion. Tourist money has given Galápagos province (the archipelago became a separate province in the early 1970s) the highest standard of living of any in Ecuador, and the Ecuadorians understandably want a part of it. But only a tiny percentage of newcomers arrive with money and skills. The vast majority are the unskilled poor, refugees from devastated, depleted farm areas or teeming urban slums. They arrive hoping to strike it rich, but most find there is no work for them and that everything—food, water, shelter, gas—costs several times the mainland price. Many stay anyway, either because they lack the return fare or because the islands, with all their problems, still offer more hope than the mainland. The population growth rate on the Galápagos today, almost

The brown pelican (Pelecanus occidentalis) is a saltwater fisher. This page, clockwise from the top: A brown pelican parent with chicks, Rábida (Jervis Island); a brown pelican in an aggressive display; brown pelicans nesting in mangroves on Punta Espinosa, Fernandina Island; Opposite page: Brown pelican nest in mangrove (top); an aggressor on the nest (bottom). Overleaf: Red-billed tropic-birds in flight (Phaeton aethreus), Tower Island.

entirely due to immigration, is twelve to fifteen percent a year; for comparison, even the fastest-growing nations on earth have rates of only three to four percent. Crime is on the rise; so are alcoholism, drug addiction, juvenile delinquency, and disease. At Academy Bay, even the shore is bare, stripped clean by the town's new poor in their search for something to eat. "In the Galápagos five years ago," one long-time resident recalls, "you never had to lock your door. Now you have to batten down everything or it disappears."

Aside from its terrible human cost, this new invasion by *Homo sapiens* frightens scientists because it has sharply accelerated the introduction of alien species. The introduced animals are of the most immediate concern, but in the long run the introduced plants may be just as harmful or worse. From the time of Bishop Berlanga's first visit until the early 1980s, botanists estimate, the total number of introduced plants was about 250. In the past five years alone, researchers at the Darwin Station have identified more than *fifty* new plants. Some are brought in as ornamentals or agricultural plants; others arrive as seeds in foodstuffs or on people's clothes, or in soil around the roots of other plants, and some of these new species are truly alarming. One recent arrival is a type of wild raspberry. With no natural predators or other biological controls, it wipes out all competing plant species and literally smothers the areas where it becomes established; in less than four years it has already taken over more than a thousand acres of San Cristóbal Island. Plants like these may not only endanger the endemic flora; where people are allowed to farm, they push out crops and smother cattle pasture that may represent the work of decades.

Recent data suggests that new organisms are arriving in huge numbers. Students have begun to sample foodstuffs and are finding them riddled with insects and arachnids. The impact of these new invertebrate arrivals, including a broad variety of fungi and disease organisms, has yet to be seen. Like the wild raspberry, these pests are not just a danger to the park—they are also a problem in agricultural zones.

The term used to describe this side of life in the islands is "chaos." Some observers go further and speak of the colonized zones as potential centers of infection, or even as fatal malignancies. It has already been over two years since Park

Director Cifuentes expressed his anxiety that Puerto Ayora had passed its population limit, with still no sign of an immigration policy and many are worried that if control is not established, they are fighting a losing battle.

On this topic, Darwin Foundation President MacFarland pulls no punches. "Every bit of good we've done will be gone," he warns, "unless two things happen: immigration must be strictly controlled and limited to those who can provide services; and a method must be put in place to quarantine and control introductions of animals and plants, including spores and seeds, and prevent transport between the islands. If anything

alive is going to be brought in, it must be proven that it is absolutely necessary to bring it, and it must be free from infection." A broad-spectrum approach is essential to prevent the introduction and spread of accidentals: inspection of all cargos, fumigation, and possibly ultraviolet or other radiation. "Whatever you need to do to make sure you're spot-checking adequately. Some still will get in, but prevention can trim it way down."

The Park Service, though, has no jurisdiction over the areas outside the park boundaries. Already pressed to its limits to handle the current flow of tourists, it would be helpless to keep out settlers in any event. On the financial side, one

This page, clockwise from top left: A green sea turtle (Chelonia mydas) lays her eggs in the nest she has dug; a Sally Lightfoot crab (Grapsus grapsus) eating a booby bird; Buccaneer Cove, on Santiago (James Island), was a favorite place for pirates to anchor in the 17th and 18th centuries. Opposite page: Aspects of Galápagos terrain showing pahoehoe-type lava formation (top) and cones (bottom). Overleaf, page left: A red-footed booby (Sula sula) on Tower Island. Overleaf page right: A red-footed booby with chick (top); a red-footed booby perched in a thicket on Tower Island (bottom).

widely discussed approach is an *ad valorem* tax on visitors, pegged to the cost of their travel within the islands, so as to be equally fair to the luxury cruise guest and the backpacker. In theory such a simple tax, wisely administered and used, could provide ample funds for the islands' municipalities, the Park Service, and the eradication program.

On the other hand, three decades of close cooperation between the Park Service and the Darwin Station staff have produced an active philosophy, succinctly embodied in the rules and regulations that are given to each visitor upon arrival. These have become a sort of Ten Commandments for the islands' management. One restriction in particular is worth quoting:

Do not leave the areas designated as visiting sites. In the more heavily used visitor sites, there are trails or areas marked with wooden stakes, within which the visitor should remain. The trails are designed to guide the visitor to all of the points of interest within a given visitor site, and at the same time to protect the resource.

If you are accustomed to hiking in places where nature is more robust, this restriction may seem as though you are being directed through a parlor filled with particularly delicate antiques. Upon reflection, the two cases may not be so different; in each, you, the intruder, are a poten-

Unlike other members of the booby family, the red-footed booby (Sula sula) tends to make its nest in bushes. This page, clockwise from the top: A red-footed booby chick in nest; a red-footed booby with chick; a red-footed booby in its brown phase; a red-footed booby on its nest. Opposite page: A red-footed booby, Tower Island. Overleaf: A red-footed booby with chick.

tially powerful agent of change—and not for the better. The final rule (there are actually fifteen altogether) puts responsibility on the visitor:

Do not hesitate to show your conservationist attitude. Explain these rules to others, and help to enforce them. Notify the National Park Service if you see any serious damage being done. You may be a decisive factor in the Islands' preservation.

"Enjoy yourself fully," the regulations conclude, "but never at the expense of what you came here to see." And since turnabout is fair play, the Park Service for its part works overtime to help make the visits interesting and rewarding; they try, for instance, to arrange for park wardens, scientists, and photographers to keep themselves and their equipment out of sight if they happen to be working near one of the land-

ing sites or trails. The idea is to not spoil the tourists' wilderness experience with unwanted glimpses of "men at work."

Nature no longer comes cheap. Operating costs for the Station now run around $450,000 a year. Most recently, at the request of the Charles Darwin Research Foundation, the Massachusetts-based Nature Conservancy has assumed a major fund-raising role. The former director of the Smithsonian Institution, S. Dillon Ripley, is heading the Galápagos Campaign Committee, whose members also include, among others, Prince Bernhard of the Netherlands, director Jean Dorst of the Paris Museum of Natural History, former president Charles J. Hedlund of Esso Middle East, and former U.S. First Lady and nature activist Lady Bird Johnson. All of which, however, still leaves the much thornier political issues. To many, it is outrageous and elitist to ask a developing country such as Ecuador, where people are literally starving, to limit the free movement of its citizens and leave a prime re-

the Station not only survived two major crises—the burning of the main administration building in 1985 and the loss of its research-transport vessel *Beagle IV*, which ran aground in the fog in August 1987—but has strengthened its scientific staff, expanded its cooperative programs with Ecuadorian universities, and begun major programs to

This page, counter-clockwise from the top right: Galápagos sea lion (Zalophus californianus wollebaeki) *leaping from the water; Galápagos penguins* (Spheniscus mendiculus) *on Fernandina Island; sea lions on beach at Española (Hood Island); penguin with Sally Lightfoot crab* (Grapsus grapsus). *Opposite page: Marine iguana* (Amblyrhynchus cristatus).

source untouched because it "belongs to the whole world." Even in the vastly more prosperous United States, any attempt to control development meets fairly stiff resistance; how, then, can environmentalists based in Washington or some European capital ask more of the Ecuadorians? But the alternative is simple. In the scientists' view, the archipelago is at the breaking point; take a *laissez-faire* approach, let the balance tip even slightly further toward unrestricted exploitation, and Galápagos could—no, *will*—soon lose everything that made it unique.

On the whole, though, the mood among those involved in Galápagos conservation is definitely upbeat. They find many causes for optimism. From 1984 to 1988, under Director Günther Reck,

eradicate wild pigs, rats, and feral dogs. A new and larger administration building has been inaugurated and construction of another new building on Isla San Cristóbal has been completed; this building will serve as a meeting and conference center and a focal point for the distribution of information about the islands. The Station recently took possession of its new research vessel, a secondhand, 46-foot-long, Maine-built motor yacht that was promptly christened the *Beagle V* and sent on the first of many conservation and science missions.

Financially, Galápagos preservation is in a chronic crisis situation, exacerbated recently by devaluation of the Ecuadorian sucre. Even so, the Foundation is probably fiscally stronger today than at any time in the past. This is thanks in part to timely gifts from the World Wide Fund for Nature, the Frankfurt Zoological Society, the Smithsonian, several major private gifts, and the donation of 40 million yen worth of video and related equipment from the government of Japan. Outgoing Executive Director Marsha E. Sitnik of the Darwin Foundation has spent the past nineteen years working for preservation of Galápagos. One reason for her long tenure, she explains, is that until recently she would have been scared to entrust the work to anyone else. "But we're financially healthier than we've ever been, and today I finally feel optimistic enough to go on to other work."

One very important new source of funding is a highly innovative program that is generally called the "debt-for-Nature swap." With funding from the World Wildlife Fund and the U.S.-based Nature Conservancy, U.S. dollars or other hard currency is used to purchase and refinance a small part of Ecuador's outstanding external debt—eight million dollars' worth so far—through the Quito-based *Fundación Natura*. This arrangement, unfortunately, has been misrepresented as just another imperialist trick by the *nortéamericano* bankers. In fact, the sucres are invested in Ecuador at current rates and the interest (also in sucres) spent within the country for such things as con-

servation programs, worker training, construction, purchase of vehicles, and preparing environmental education materials.

An even more hopeful sign was seen in 1988, when the leaders of all the country's major political groups met in Quito with the heads of the national agencies Dituris (tourism) and Ingala (Galápagos development) and the minister of ag-

The Galápagos Islands were so named in the 17th century after the Spanish word for the giant tortoise, galápago. This page, clockwise from the top: giant tortoise feeding; tortoise (Geochelone elephantopus vandenburghi), Isabela Island; tortoise drinking. Opposite page: Tortoise on Santa Cruz Island (top); this tortoise may weigh up to 600 lbs (bottom).

This page, top: Tortoise (Geochelone elephantopus) at Alcedo, Isabela Island.

Bottom: A conflict between tortoises arises. Opposite page: This photograph con- *veys both the size and age that can be reached by the Galápagos tortoise (top); tortoises* *trudge through the mud and fog at Santa Cruz Island (bottom).*

As with other species in the Galápagos archipelago, the giant tortoise (Geochelone elephantopus) diversified in order to adapt to the particular environment of the island it inhabited. Clockwise from top: Tortoise feeding; a tortoise in the underbrush of Santa Cruz Island; tortoise at Alcedo, Isabela Island; tortoise at Española (Hood Island). Opposite page: A saddleback tortoise on Española (Hood Island), top; a giant tortoise at Santa Cruz Island (bottom). Overleaf: A red-billed tropic-bird (Phaeton aetherus) in flight.

protected areas. "The Galápagos was chosen as the workshop site," noted Dr. Daniel Evans, the Darwin Station's new director, "to allow participants from all over Latin America to learn from our unique working arrangement."

If the archipelago survives in good ecological health, it will be a tribute above all the extraordinary passion and perseverance of a handful of underpaid, often unappreciated professionals. And the islands themselves seems to bring out the best and most intense qualities in its naturalist guests. To explore the Galápagos, world-renowned ornithologist Roger Tory Peterson has endured with (reasonable) cheerfulness being terrorized by a bull sea lion and bitten on the leg by a giant tortoise. The eminent Harvard evolutionist George Gaylord Simpson, 71 years-old and seriously ill during a cruise in the islands, had the ship's personnel literally carry him off and on the ship rather than miss a chance to see Galápagos penguins nesting on Isabela. (He learned later that he had been suffering from lobar pneumonia, and that the excursion could easily have cost him his life.)

Thanks to such dedication, there is better hope for the Galápagos today than for almost any

riculture (whose domain includes the National Park Service) to explore the issues affecting the islands' future. Until recently, it was generally accepted that getting the Ecuadorian authorities to control movement in and out of the islands would be politically impossible. As one observer put it, "No official is ready yet to confront the political powder keg of setting an immigration

Darwin Research Station and the Galápagos National Park Service serves as a model for such interagency collaboration. In March 1989, the Latin American Office of the United Nations' Food and Agricultural Organization (FAO), through its Project for Management of Wildlife, National Parks and Protected Areas, sponsored an international workshop in the Galápagos on research in

quota for mainlanders wishing to settle in the Galápagos." But the response at the 1988 meeting, by all accounts, was unanimous: the situation is indeed critical and it is time to act. Meanwhile, a Galápagos grassroots group, including the mayors of the archipelago's eight towns, the governor of Galápagos Province, and the regional education supervisor were planning a position paper that would concisely explain the archipelago's problems and offer suggested actions, to be presented to congress for action in the summer of 1989.

The close collaboration between the Charles

"... there must," wrote Darwin, "be in the whole archipelago at least two thousand craters." This page, top: A sunset in the Galápagos Islands. Bottom: Pahoehoe-type lava formations at Santiago (James Island). Opposite page: Aerial views of Beagle Crater at Isabela Island (top) and Sombrero Chino crater, near Santiago (James Island). Overleaf: A blue shark (Prionace glauca) cuts through the water. Blue sharks have worldwide distribution.

ditions; things might have been much worse if the ship had sunk in Tagus Cove or another bay with limited water circulation. Optimists like to point out that the hull of the *Iguana*, which stuck up prominently above water through the latter half of 1988, is slowly settling into the bottom and will soon evolve into an excellent diving reef!

The Galápagos' water boundaries still form a protective moat, keeping away numerous would-be invaders. (In an era of global warming, it is comforting to know that the ocean's temperature-moderating effect offers some degree of protection against the so-called "greenhouse effect.") In April 1987, all the archipelago's inshore waters and all waters extending 15 miles off the outer coast of the islands were declared a Marine Reserve—the result of a visit by Ecuador's President Cordero to the islands and the biologists who work there. There are still problems—in particular, longlining for shark by the Japanese is said by reliable sources to be killing other fish, including jack, mackerel and tuna, in large numbers—but, as James Cribb observed, it is a "first step in the conservation of one of the planet's most exotic and magical environments."

In his student days, marine biologist Jack Grove first went to the Galápagos as a deckhand on a sailboat. He felt inspired by swimming with large and in some cases commercially important fishes that had no fear of man. One type of grouper, related to the sea bass, was known lo-

other major wilderness area in the Third World. Over much of the archipelago the original ecosystems, though impoverished, are still fundamentally intact; if the alien species—such as the goats on Santa Fé and Pinta—are eradicated, the endemic vegetation and animals are often capable of making a dramatic comeback. The archipelago has even survived its first major oil spill, when the foundering *Iguana* dumped 50,000 gallons of diesel oil into Academy Bay. Luckily, the hot weather, strong sunlight, and wave action were enough to quickly restore normal con-

This page, counter-clockwise from top: A hardy plant colonizes the bare lava at Isabela Island; on Fernandina Island, the land iguana (Conolophus subcristatus) migrates to the volcano's rim to nest; a Galápagos hawk (Buteo galapagoensis) on Isabela Island; one of Bainbridge Rocks (Islands), with Santiago (James Island) in the background. Opposite page: a lava heron (Butorides sundevalli) fishing.

cally as *norteño*. Fishermen in the Galápagos had been catching it for years with hook and line, but Grove was the first person to pay it the courtesy of a full scientific description. "Our philosophy," he insists, "should be to enter these environments as an observer, and not as a predator."

On the purely commercial level, the Galápagos Islands are valued for their remoteness and the exotic life forms that make them a fascinating tourist destination. The same qualities make them a priceless resource for science as well. But on what might be called a philosophical or spiritual level, they have another value. The archipelago remains one of the few unaltered microsystems in the world, and the world needs to have such places. Or perhaps it is simply that we need to preserve Galápagos as an act of faith.

A hundred and fifty-four years ago, the Galápagos helped Darwin find the key to evolution, and thereby became a symbol of our intellectual mastery of nature. In our time, the Islands are destined to become a new symbol: either of our heedless, continuing plunder of the planet; or, if we are lucky, of our growing ability and determination to coexist in harmony with the natural world.

INDEX OF PHOTOGRAPHERS

Photographer	Page Number
The map illustration which appears on pages 6-7 is by Tony Gibbons, courtesy of Bernard Thornton Artists, London.	
Walt Anderson	8, 12 center right, 21 top & bottom right, 43 bottom left, 50, 51 top right, 64 top, 66 center left, 70 bottom left & bottom right, 91 bottom right, 101 center left, 103, 111 bottom left & bottom right, 116, 123 bottom right, 130 bottom left, 132 top left & center right, 156 bottom, 163 center right, 179 top.
Frederick D. Atwood	9 top right, 10 top, 10 bottom left, 12 top left, 27 bottom right, 31 center right, 51 bottom right, 48, 52 bottom left, 54-55, 58, 59 center left, 61, 65 bottom, 67 bottom, 68 bottom, 69 bottom right, 88 bottom right, 105 top left, 108 center & bottom left, 109 bottom, 118 bottom, 122 bottom, 126 top right, 130 top left & top right, 132 bottom left, 141 top, 147 top, 150 top left, 164 center right, 165 bottom, 169 bottom, 180 top, 183 bottom right.
Erwin & Peggy Bauer	3, 38 top right, 41, 47 top right, 49 bottom left, 60 bottom left, 71, 89 top, 91 center left, 101 center right, 105 center, 123 bottom left, 132 center left, 142 center, 151, 183 bottom left.
Doug Cheeseman	34 bottom left, 38 top left, 49 center, 64 bottom right, 66 bottom, 108 bottom right, 130 bottom right, 154, 173 top left, 174-175, 178 bottom right.
Ted Cheeseman	51 center, 69 center & bottom left, 171 top, 173 center left.
Buff Corsi	56 bottom left, 69 top, 146 bottom right, 147 bottom, 152, 159 top left, 166-167, 173 bottom.
Gerald Corsi	11, 17 center left, 26, 27 bottom left, 51, top left, 88 bottom left, 90, 91 top right, 95 center right, 100, 102, 104 bottom, 118 center left, 119, 123 top right, 126 bottom left, 127, 128-129, 131, 133 bottom, 134-135, 148, 150 bottom, 156 top, 158 top, 161, 164 top, 170.
Gerald & Buff Corsi	27 top, 32 bottom right, 38 bottom left, 40 top, 47 bottom left, 52 bottom right, 56 top & bottom right, 60 top, 64 bottom left, 88 top left, 95 top left & bottom left, 97 bottom right, 110 top, 115 top left, 117 top, 118 top right, 121 bottom, 125 top, 146 top left, 149 bottom, 157, 159 center right & bottom right.
Josh Feingold	14 top, 15 top, 31 top right, 33, 59 bottom, 76 bottom, 85 bottom right, 95 center left, 104 top, 106-107, 121 top, 140 top, 142 top right & bottom left, 146 bottom left, 155 bottom left, 158 bottom, 162 top, 187 top.
The Image Bank/Paolo Gori	184-185.
The Image Bank/ John Netherton	10 center left, 12 bottom left, 16 center right & bottom, 20 bottom, 24 top, 28-29, 32 top, 38 bottom right, 39 bottom, 40 bottom, 43 top, 44-45, 49 top & bottom right, 65 top, 72-73, 108 top right, 109 top, 110 bottom, 111 top, 114 top, 115 bottom right, 120, 138-139, 143 bottom, 150 center, 169 top, 171 bottom.
The Image Bank/Allan Seiden	60 bottom right, 136 top, 162 bottom.
Ted Levin	16 top, 31 center left, 53, 96, 105 bottom right, 123 top left, 136 bottom left.
Natural Science Photos/ Fiona Bass	34 top, 35 (2), 36-37.
PhotoEdit/Jack Stein Grove	9 top left, 17 top, 21 center left, 24 bottom, 118 center right.
PhotoEdit/Anna Zuckerman	42, 97 bottom left, 122 top.
Laura Riley	13 bottom, 16 center left, 17 bottom, 21 center right, 31 top left, 47 top left, 52 top, 57, 59 top & center right, 94, 101 top right, 114 bottom, 115 top right & bottom left, 126 bottom right, 149 top, 155 top left, 180 bottom, 183 top left, 187 center left.
Peter Salwen	34 bottom right, 98-99, 143 top.
Marty Snyderman	14 center, 15 bottom, 20 top, 74 (4), 75 (2), 76 top, 77-84*, 85 top left & bottom left, 86 (3), 87 (2), 133 top, 153, 160 bottom, 178 top right, 179 bottom, 188-189.
Survival Anglia/Jeff Foott	66 top, 67 top.
Survival Anglia/Sylvia Harcourt	12 top right, 13 top, 30, 66 center right, 68 top, 101 bottom left, 137, 140 bottom, 160 top, 178 center left.
Survival Anglia/Dr. F. Köster	39 top, 46, 47 bottom right, 91 bottom left, 117 bottom, 155 bottom right.
Survival Anglia/ Dieter & Mary Plage	4-5, 14 bottom, 18-19, 22 (3), 23 (2), 25 (2), 43 bottom right, 70 top, 88 top right, 89 bottom, 97 top, 112-113, 124 (4), 125 bottom left & bottom right, 141 bottom, 142 bottom right, 146 top right, 163 center left & bottom left, 168 top left & top right, 172, 176, 177 (4), 181 (2), 182 top, 186, 186 (2), 187 bottom, 190, 191 (4).
Survival Anglia/Alan Root	144-145.
Survival Anglia/Maurice Tibbles	173 center right.
Stephen Trimble	9 bottom, 10 center right, 27 center right, 32 bottom left, 62-63, 92-93, 136 bottom right, 164 center left, 165 top, 168 bottom, 182 bottom, 183 center right.

* All photographs which appear on these pages are by this photographer.